Action Research: Principles and Practice

D0060795

Since its first publication in 1988, *Action Research: Principles and Practice* has become a key text in its field. Interest in this area has developed considerably in recent years, making this updated edition a timely contribution.

Jean McNiff clearly describes and explains the practices of action research and its underlying values. She urges education professionals to become reflective practitioners by conducting their own self-study and holding themselves accountable for their own influence. This second edition also includes:

- new case-study material
- additional chapters on the educational significance of action research
- an overview of current methodological discussion

Educators planning research in their own work settings will find this book a helpful introduction to the subject while those studying on higher degree courses will find it an indispensable resource.

The book is a valuable addition to the literature on research methods in education and contributes to contemporary debates about the generation and dissemination of knowledge and its potential influence for wider social contexts.

Jean McNiff is an independent researcher and consultant, and a Distinguished Scholar in Residence at the University of Limerick. She has written widely on action research in education. Her books include *Your and Your Action Research Project* (1996, written with Pam Lomax and Jack Whitehead) and *Action Research in Organisations* (2000, with Jack Whitehead), both published by Routledge. You can reach her on http://www.jeanmcniff.com

Jack Whitehead is a lecturer in education at the University of Bath. He is a former President of the British Educational Research Association, a Distinguished Scholar in Residence at Westminster College, Utah, and Visiting Professor at Brock University, Ontario. His work on living educational theory and the use of embodied values as living standards of practice and judgement can be accessed at http://www.actionresearch.net

Action Research: Principles and Practice

Second Edition

Jean McNiff
with
Jack Whitehead

London and New York

First published 2002
by RoutledgeFalmer
11 New Fetter Lane, London EC4P 4EE

Simultaneously published in the USA and Canada
by RoutledgeFalmer
29 West 35th Street, New York, NY 10001

Reprinted 2003

RoutledgeFalmer is an imprint of the Taylor & Francis Group

© 2002 Jean McNiff, Jack Whitehead

Typeset in Times by
Keystroke, Jacaranda Lodge, Wolverhampton
Printed and bound in Great Britain by
MPG Books Ltd, Bodmin, Cornwall

All rights reserved. No part of this book may be reprinted or
reproduced or utilised in any form or by any electronic,
mechanical, or other means, now known or hereafter
invented, including photocopying and recording, or in any
information storage or retrieval system, without permission in
writing from the publishers.

British Library Cataloguing in Publication Data
A catalogue record for this book is available
from the British Library

Library of Congress Cataloguing in Publication Data
McNiff, Jean.
    Action research : principles and practice / Jean McNiff with
    Jack Whitehead.—2nd ed.
        p. cm.
    Includes bibliographical references and index.
    1. Action research in education. 2. Action research—Methodology.
    I. Whitehead, Jack. II. Title.
    LB1028.24 .M398 2001
    370′.7′2—dc21
    2001031911

ISBN 0–415–21994–9

Contents

Figures

Acknowledgements

We acknowledge with gratitude permission to reprint the following diagrams:

Figure 3.3: 'The individual aspect in action research', from Stephen Kemmis and Robin McTaggart (eds), *The Action Research Planner* (3rd edn, Deakin University 1988)

Figure 3.4: 'A revised version of Lewin's model of action research', from John Elliott, *Action Research for Educational Change* (Open University Press 1991).

Preface

The ideas in this book have been informed by three main influences: my work experience over the last ten years; my learning partnership with Jack Whitehead; and the educative influence of Noam Chomsky. During those years I have been working, mostly in Ireland and Northern Ireland, organising and teaching professional development courses. The people who come on these courses are mainly teachers, but include also administrators, business managers, members of religious orders, clerical staff and others – all experienced people working in education contexts who want to look critically at their work and work situations with a view to improving them. The courses lead to the awards of MA, MPhil and PhD; they are awarded by British universities. At the same time I have maintained close contact with Jack Whitehead, who works at the University of Bath. We share a common commitment to popularising a form of theory which is located in the descriptions and explanations people produce for their work and which constitute their own living educational theories (Whitehead, 1989). The dialogical form of this book shows the nature of our own learning and knowledge-creating process.

A story of Ireland

I first began my work in Ireland as a consultant with a small private college in Dublin. The action research inservice initiatives we offered were attractive to serving teachers, and we approached Irish universities to see if they would accredit the work. These overtures were unsuccessful, so we approached British universities, one of whom agreed to support the development of the initiative as a practitioner-research-based modular programme. Because of its own internal reconfigurations (possibly for other reasons), the Dublin college decided after two years not to continue with the initiative, so they and I parted company. I then had to decide whether I would go it alone. In terms of my educational and political values it was not a hard decision; the upheaval it meant in my personal life was something else.

The British university and I agreed that I would be appointed as a part-time lecturer to bring the studies of the first group to successful closure. On their graduation (thirty-one people) the university then allowed me to support a second group (forty-five people). Now I worked as an independent researcher appointed by the university to develop the work.

In the meantime I negotiated with another British university to develop a guided doctorate programme. My current scenario, therefore, is that I am in partnership with one university for the development of MA courses, and in partnership with another for MPhil/PhD degrees. As well as working with groups aiming for accreditation, I have taught hundreds of other people by running short courses or doing presentations in a wide variety of education contexts.

Action research is now high profile in Ireland, and people have made it their own (see, for example, Condren, 2000; Lillis, 2000b). This is how leadership should work. Good leaders should create opportunities for people to shine and then get out of the way and let them do so, while continually providing background practical and emotional support.

The experience has been rewarding but difficult, and has resulted in significant learning (McNiff, 2000). In terms of this book, it has brought home just how difficult it is for people to be action researchers in a lived sense, to want to create their own identities and change their own situations in the face of sometimes entrenched hostile attitudes. I have learnt how to deal with the truth of power, to negotiate my way through the complexities of institutional power-constituted epistemologies, and to resist attempts to persuade me to go away. I have also learnt what amazing change can be generated for social good when people take responsibility for their own work and decide to improve unsatisfactory situations.

When I wrote the first edition I did so from the limited experience of doing action research within my home and work situations and my own PhD programme. This edition is written from the wider perspective of doing action research within the problematics of trying to renegotiate the knowledge base of professional learning within national policy-making contexts, and of engaging with powerful institutional forces who want to prevent critiques from translating into a destabilisation of established systems of knowledge. It is written out of the experience of encouraging people to challenge their own prejudices and the prejudices of others, and of providing emotional and practical support when they inevitably run up against resistance, both from their own conditioned ways of knowing and from the establishment. Together, these colleagues and I have created a force for education, a group of people who see the potential for educational change and systematically work towards it. While we do not claim to represent a coherent or oppositional voice, we do by implication criticise axiomatic systems of knowledge, and try to influence institutional managers to rethink policy in light of the significant body of research-based evidence which now exists in seventy validated masters dissertations, with more on the way.

A story of Bath

Jack Whitehead and I first became acquainted in 1981 when I enrolled as a part-time doctoral candidate under his supervision. I received my award in 1989. Since then, Jack and I have developed a special learning relationship.

Jack's ideas about the creative nature of knowledge and knowledge generation have been a major influence in my personal and professional life. His ideas have provided the methodological and epistemological basis for the work in Ireland (see McNiff and Collins, 1994; Collins and McNiff, 1999; see also the collections of dissertations which are to be found on Jack's and my websites, www.action research.net and www.jeanmcniff.com). One of the reasons for the success of our work as course providers and educational leaders is the nature of our own educative relationship. We not only help and challenge each other to think creatively and to critique our own and each other's ideas but also help each other to keep going in the face of much institutional indifference and hostility. In new work (Whitehead, forthcoming) Jack is showing how supportive relationships such as ours are central in the creation of learning communities. People's learning can change their social and institutional contexts, and people can learn in and through educative relationships, so it follows that a major task of educational researchers is to generate knowledge about how educational knowledge is produced within and through relationships and which kinds of relationship are necessary for this process. This is a key issue both for Jack and myself. In this book I am hoping to show the nature of the relationships as they are manifested in colleagues' explanations for why they feel they have learnt well and how their learning might affect the futures of other people for whom they are responsible.

The educative influence of Noam Chomsky

I first encountered the ideas of Noam Chomsky when I studied for a masters degree in applied linguistics. I was captivated by his ideas about the generative transformational nature of language, its acquisition and development, and how these ideas were embedded within issues concerning the nature of knowledge, its acquisition and development. When I began to develop my commitments to supporting practitioners in undertaking their action enquiries I also got to grips with Noam's political theories, about the need to respect pluralistic practices in the creation of good social orders, and the responsibility of intellectuals to tell the truth and expose lies (Chomsky, 1966). I began to understand my responsibility as an educator to arrange spaces for people to create their own mutually negotiated identities. I took heart from Noam's indomitable courage and tenacity. I met with him some years ago, and I reflect frequently on his comment, 'If they are trying to ignore you, you must be doing something right.' 'They', for me, are the elites whose interests are served by promoting traditional scholarships and epistemologies and whose values include the selfish accumulation of power and wealth with which they close down opportunities for others' learning. In spite of 'them', ideas about practitioner action research are now firmly embedded within the culture of my main work context (Government of Ireland, 1998, 1999a, 1999b). Noam and I continue to connect, and I benefit from his kindness and support.

Jean McNiff
March 2001

The eyes of the Lord keep watch over knowledge.
Proverbs 22:12

Introduction

A great deal has happened since the publication of the first edition of this book in 1988, both in the world of action research and in my own learning.

In 1988 action research was still struggling for legitimacy. Today it is recognised as a valid form of enquiry, with its own methodologies and epistemologies, its own criteria and standards of judgement. Debates still take place about the nature of action research, how people carry out their research and for what purposes, but there is general agreement that action research has an identity of its own and should not be spoken about in terms of traditional forms of research.

This book is a report of the action research I have engaged in since 1988. It sets out what I have learnt, how my learning has developed, and what I hope to learn in future. I have learnt about action research through doing action research.

Through studying my practice as a professional educator I have become aware that the heart of the matter is to do with how I can contribute to the development of a good social order through education. This has meant spending time trying to understand the nature of a good order, and how it might be created; engaging with substantive issues such as freedom, pluralism and social justice, and with methodological issues such as how knowledge is created and disseminated. Increasingly I have come to understand the importance of Plato's question of how it might be possible to hold the one and the many together at the same time (see p. 5). I can now show how, over the years, I have undertaken focused research projects within the broader research project of working towards a good order, and how I have come to reconceptualise the nature of action research as a problematic process of coming to know rather than as a pathway to right knowledge.

It is good research practice to take stock from time to time in order to decide how to move forward. For example, the American Educational Research Association took as its 2001 theme the questions 'What do we know? How do we know it?' I want to ask the same kinds of questions here in relation to my own learning. This will inevitably involve testing my own ideas against theories in the literature. I am asking, 'What do I know? How have I come to know it? How do I validate my knowledge? How can I share my knowledge? What will I use my knowledge for?' These questions also act as organising principles throughout.

A key aspect of my enquiry has been to come to understand the importance of critiquing the assumptions that underlie my own ideas and practice. I like the following comment by Michael Young. Speaking in the context of curriculum change, he says, 'if teachers subject the assumptions underlying their practices to critical examination, they will understand how to change the curriculum' (Young, 1998: 27). The same holds in the development of ideas. If researchers try to understand the assumptions underlying their theories, they might come to understand how and why to critique and improve them.

I am now aware of the assumptions that underlie my ideas and practice. This statement would not have been true when I wrote the first edition. I have become critical, and I try to influence others also to become critical, because I believe that criticism is essential for generating non-coercive knowledge in the creation of good social orders. Edward Said (1991: 28) says it well:

> I take criticism so seriously as to believe that, even in the very midst of a battle in which one is unmistakably on one side against another, there should be criticism, because there must be critical consciousness if there are to be issues, problems, values, even lives to be fought for.

Today I understand my practice better than I did before, both as a professional educator and as a theorist. I understand what I am doing, and how and why I am doing it.

In the first edition I was mainly interested in the procedures of action research. During the 1980s I had been incorporating action research into my practice as a secondary teacher of personal and social education. While I wrote about action research as a creative and spontaneous process, this was a belief expressed from within the safe and secure context of researching in my own back yard. I had not at that point begun supporting others in doing their action research, or indeed doing it myself in a problematic context. This has all changed.

For ten years now I have been working with educators across the professions, mainly in Ireland, supporting them in gaining accreditation for studying their own workplace practice. I have learnt my job on the job. I have actively researched my own practice to help me learn about it and be effective, and I have consistently evaluated and produced reports of how my developing understanding influences my work with others, as I am doing here (see, for example, McNiff, 2000; McNiff and Collins, 1994); and I have encouraged others to do the same (see, for example, Collins and McNiff, 1999; Lillis, 2000a).

I therefore want to present some key learnings, and show how they have arisen from studying my practice and testing the ideas against theories in the literature. These learnings in turn have generated new learnings and new practices.

Key learnings

Freedom and agonistic pluralism

I have come to appreciate the centrality of the idea of freedom in my life. I relate to Roger Hausheer's account of how freedom became a core principle in Isaiah Berlin's philosophy: 'we are free beings in some absolutely non-deterministic sense.

So basic is this conviction that our entire moral vocabulary rests upon it: notions such as responsibility, praise, remorse and desert stand or fall with it' (Berlin, 1998: xxviii). Freedom has come to be a core value for me, possibly because through studying my practice I realise how unfree I have been. Until quite recently I have felt constrained to be the person other people have wished me to be. That is no longer the case. I have learnt that I can make choices, and can create myself as the self I want to be, insofar as I am unencumbered by my biological make-up, history, gender, and other elements of social situatedness. Choices, however, always involve trade-offs, and I have learnt how important it is to choose wisely and to help others to do the same with due regard to the consequences of choices. I have also come to appreciate how privileged I am to be in a position where I can make choices about my own life. I remain professionally independent, and am able to think and express my ideas freely. Few people are so privileged, and I am deeply aware of my responsibility to use my privilege to help those who do not have the same opportunities.

I have learnt from Berlin, and from the work of John Gray, who has also been influenced by Berlin's thought, how important it is to link the idea of freedom with pluralism, recognising that pluralism does not necessarily mean trying to reconcile conflicting views, but means engaging with conflict. People will always be in conflict to some degree, says Berlin. Nor is there a universal overarching structure of values whereby conflict can be resolved. It is by working with conflict that we come to understand and accommodate one another's differences (I explore these ideas further in Chapter 13). Gray calls this idea 'agonistic pluralism'; *agon* is a Greek word 'whose meaning covers both competition or rivalry and the conflicts of characters in tragic drama' (Gray, 1995a: 1). These ideas have become central to my thinking about action research. Contrary to what I thought in 1988, action research does not refer to a methodology that leads to harmonious thought and action but to a problematic practice of coming to know through struggle. My own learning has developed as part of the struggle to understand.

Importantly, therefore, like Mellor (1998), I have come to see action research not as a specific pathway but as a form of problematic practice. Referring to Schön's metaphor of the swampy lowlands of practical life (see p. 20), Mellor says: 'I eventually came to accept that my struggle in the swamp *was* the method, not a path to find a better method' (1998: 462; my emphasis). I have come to the same understanding: research is as much about the process of answering questions as it is about the answers themselves. Sometimes it is impossible to find an answer, and we just do the best with what we have.

The need for dialectical forms of theory in understanding practice

I have come to see the severe limitations of dominant approaches to human enquiry. Berlin has again been helpful. Most approaches to human enquiry, he says, regard it as an unproblematic unity. This approach is mistaken. History, for example, is not the telling of one unified story by one-who-knows, but an accumulation of multiple stories, told by people themselves, and these people all share different views, hopes and visions (Berlin, 1998). Berlin explains how Vico (see Vico, 1999) felt the same with regard to the evolution of science as a cultural phenomenon: each culture has its own understanding of the world in which it lives. To try to present the diversity and richness of human living as a straightforward story, as well as to gloss over the fact that people seldom share the same values base and are potentially always in conflict, is to deny the importance for social evolution of the need for people to recognise one another as human beings able to think for themselves, and the need to live in ways which respect pluralism and independence of mind and action.

These ideas have strengthened concerns long held by my colleague Jack Whitehead, myself and those whom we support about the kind of theory appropriate to studying education and learning (see, for example, Whitehead, 1989). I have come to critique dominant theories which present learning as all of a kind. These theories speak *about* learning as an object of study. The same trend is evident in much contemporary work on action research. Action research and people's practices are spoken about; they are presented as abstractions, objects of study, not as real-world practices.

Such approaches are contradictory in two respects: first, accounts are presented about human enquiry as a unified and unproblematic phenomenon; second, the accounts are presented from an externalist perspective. I have come to see instead the importance of presenting accounts of practice to show its inherently unstable and problematic nature; and why these accounts should be presented by people themselves. In other words, I have come to understand the reasons for using a dialectical, rather than a propositional, form of logic to understand educational enquiry (see below, p. 5).

I am interested in why many theorists do not see the need to produce live evidence to show how their theories have improved the quality of their own or other people's lives, and why they prefer to stay with conceptual theoretical models. Bourdieu's ideas have been helpful; he says (1990) that for many people the model is more important than the reality it is aiming to represent. I think I understand better why this is the case, and will speak of this issue throughout.

The need for a logic of practice

Supporting practitioners as they engage with their enquiries and learn about their work, and becoming deeply involved in learning about mine, has helped me to see that generating theories about work has to begin within the work. It is no use importing preconceived ideas of how practice will fall out; things simply do not work like that. Creating ideas begins with practice, and is located within the practice. As the practice evolves, so too does the theory. It is important to critique one's own theory against the wider theories in the literature, but it seems self-evident that the kind of theory which will help us improve our social situations has to arise from learning about the practice from within the practice itself (this is not, however, to deny that propositional theories can provide valuable insights which can be integrated within our logics of practice).

This view is quite contrary to the dominant opinion that an empirical body of knowledge exists which can be applied to practice. If I am honest, I saw action research like this when I wrote the first edition. I was still caught up in my own traditional system of knowledge which I had internalised from being part of it as a student and then as a teacher. Even though I was doing action research I still had not worked out an adequate theory of what I was doing. That took an inordinately long time, about ten years of work as a professional educator, and the understanding grew out of the process of writing and evaluating as much as out of the workplace practice. I learned through teaching. This experience also reinforced for me how important it is to stick with a felt need that something is worth investigating, even though one is not sure what it is, and to know that the answer will emerge over time if one is true to that sense of enquiry.

The value of uncertainty

I have let go of the need for certainty. I am therefore seemingly stuck with a philosophical paradox: I have become certain of the need for uncertainty. I live easily with the paradox. The one thing I, like Descartes, can be certain of is life itself. Life is unpredictable, surprising, creative, self-transforming; an implicate order underpins all (Bohm and Peat, 2000), and this order is generative and transformational. This also is the nature of my practice, as part of life (McNiff, 2000). I am certain that life and my practice are evolutionary and move towards life-affirming forms; my certainty and uncertainty are complementary, not contradictory. This ability to hold two seemingly contradictory elements together is a feature of the dialectical kind of theory mentioned above, a form of theory which goes beyond the linear propositional Aristotelian logic beloved of many theorists of education (for example, Pring, 2000). Propositional logic attempts to eliminate contradiction from human enquiry while dialectical logic embraces the idea that human living is full of contradictions.

I have come to appreciate the need for confidence in uncertainty in professional development contexts. When I first began my work as a professional educator in the early 1990s I held as a main research purpose the quest for certainty. It was my responsibility to make sure course members got on to the right path and stayed on it. I also felt responsible for the way they thought. Over the years, however, I have come to see my work as encouraging people to develop confidence in their own independence of mind and spirit, to play with new ideas, to challenge me, and to resist all efforts by others in their social contexts to bring their thinking to closure. My work is to encourage them to become aware of how they learn, and to use their knowledge to improve their own social situations.

My certainty of the value of uncertainty now travels to a current interest about the kind of theory most appropriate for explaining the potential of action research as a way of learning about one's practice, and as a power for personal and social renewal. This point is a key issue of this book. What is not at issue is a definition of action research; many definitions of action research are to be found in the literature. What *is* at issue is the form of theory used to describe and explain action research processes, the whole business of whether we regard human enquiry as an objective phenomenon which we observe from a distance or as a living process of which we are part.

How identity can be manufactured

I have learnt how one group often tries to colonise and manufacture the identities of another. In *Orientalism* (1995) Edward Said explains how Orientalism is a concept created by Occidental men (and indeed how social categories themselves are fabricated). Orientalism is generally understood in terms of white male Western middle-class experience. The same practice of colonisation is today visible in the world of action research. Dominant theories of action research are manufactured mainly by intellectuals located in higher-education institutional contexts.* Little concern is expressed about how action research might be used to gather and test evidence to show possible improvement in the quality of practice, their own or anybody else's. Theory generation becomes an end in itself, separated from social purpose. However, other voices are now to be heard (for example, Atkinson, 2000; Hamilton, 1998). The approach developed by Jack Whitehead, myself and others has encouraged researchers like these to offer their personal theories of practice to show how they improved their own understanding and action in a given situation. We think it is important to produce real world stories of improved practice, and to show how our educative influence has had some effect in wider contexts.

My report on knowledge

This book, then, is a formative research report, my own report on knowledge (Lyotard, 1984) from two perspectives. The first is how I theorise my practice as an educator. Because I continually assess the validity of my ideas and critique them against those of others, my self-evaluation also involves a second perspective of how action research is theorised in contemporary work. I am aware of some slippage between my ideas and others in the literature, and I want to explore the nature of the slippage.

I am particularly concerned about some trends which I feel are turning action research into a set of techniques, an oppressive technology which denies the humanitarian and egalitarian ideologies that inspired the action research movement in the first place. I think there is a better way. This opinion is informed by the empirical evidence produced by the communities of action researchers with whom I am fortunate to associate. These researchers are generating a living form of theory

---

* There is, however, clear concern about this situation in some quarters, notably from the editors of *Educational Action Research*. They frequently call for more accounts by practitioners not in higher educational contexts. One wonders what is going on that such accounts do not often appear.

(Whitehead, 1989; www.actionresearch.net) by studying their own practice. The descriptions and explanations they are producing for their own work show how they are improving the quality of educational experience within workplaces, and the significance of their work for personal and institutional improvement. The communities of practitioners I support in Ireland are changing what counts as educational knowledge (see, for example, Nugent, 2000; O'Shea, 2000).

Structure and content of this report

Within the report I follow accepted conventions in that I set out my research question, explain the background of the research and its present contexts, identify a research design, show how I gather data and turn it into evidence by setting criteria for success, validate the evidence, and indicate new directions for research. I attempt to show the development of the ideas through the developmental form of the text, as I ask questions of the kind (see Whitehead, 1993):

- What is my concern?
- Why am I concerned?
- What do I think I can do about it?
- What will I do?
- How will I be able to show whether I am influencing the situation for good?
- How will I judge whether any conclusions I come to are reasonably fair and accurate?
- What will I do then?

Developments since the first edition

The widening vistas of action research

Major developments have taken place in the contexts in which action research is practised, and in the refinement of its methodologies. Perhaps the most obvious development has been the rapid spread of action research across the professions. It is now a worldwide phenomenon (Noffke, 1997a), and has moved beyond the teaching profession where it originally came to prominence. However, it is still located primarily in the field of education in a variety of contexts, and its theorists include people involved in the education of adults, young people, workplace practitioners, community participants, professionals, Third Agers and others.

The educational values base of action research

The values base of action research has become central. Increasingly researchers are explaining how action research aims to be a living out of values (see Whitehead, 1985 for seminal work). Some writers, however, do not see the need to do this. Carson and Sumara (1997), for example, write about action research as a lived practice but do not show their own lived practice within the work. In Whitehead's words, they would be the 'living contradictions' who subscribe to a value in principle but fail to live the value in practice. Mark Hadfield (1998) has written a persuasive critique of the text.

Living forms of theory

A tension exists between those who produce abstract theories about practice and those who produce personal theories from within practice. The tendency for the abstract theorists is still to talk about practice as a thing 'out there' rather than showing their own engagement with action research processes.

This willingness to stay at the level of linguistic abstraction is a pertinent issue. Linguistic analysis is often considered appropriate and sufficient for communicating the meaning of what we are doing. Faith in words and static models permeates the culture. For example, in relation to the assessment of professional practice, it is often considered sufficient to show a person's capacity to do a job by filling in a 'can do' checklist. The evidence for professional competence is a tick in a box. In this view, it is possible to score 100 per cent on a management or teaching profile without demonstrating that one can manage or teach in practice.

On the other hand, a person's capacity to do a job can be judged in terms of whether they improved the quality of somebody else's educational experience, and whether they can support their claim that they did so. The evidence will be assessed in terms of identified success criteria, and these are related to the practitioner's educational values and purposes. Did they help others to think and act for themselves? Did they inspire others to take responsibility for their own work? Can they produce evidence in terms of the real-life experiences of those whose lives they influenced?

The issue arises whether it is possible to show a link between abstract theory and personal practical theory, and how this can be done. Abstract forms of thinking are usually represented linguistically and through inert models. Criteria and outcomes are presented and analysed in conceptual terms. Words and marks on paper count, not actions. On the other hand, personal theories are produced from within practice. Criteria and outcomes are presented and analysed in terms of the quality of practice, particularly the relationships among people. The accounts of practice may be presented linguistically, but the words have to show the lived reality of practice and how it is impacting on others. Multimedia forms of presentation using digital technologies are important aids in this process (see www.actionresearch.net).

The meanings of our lives

The tensions spill over into how we give meaning to our lives.

Some people believe meaning is a matter of looking up definitions in a dictionary. This does not get us very far in understanding values-based living, especially when we accept that values are always potentially in conflict in pluralistic societies.

Education, for example, is traditionally taken to be an interaction, usually between people, which leads to learning and growth. The use of only linguistic definitions, however, does not always communicate how concepts such as education are understood as real-life processes. Hitler's *Mein Kampf* contained a theory of education which was accepted by his culture, but his view was quite different from the one expressed in Dewey's *Democracy and Education*. The same principle applies to words such as learning, development and many other potentially value-laden concepts. Words remain words; they represent reality but they are not the reality they represent. We learn to bully as much as we learn to care – both tendencies are in our make-up. A war can develop as much as a peace process. Linguistic meanings do not always communicate how we try to live our lives. It is important, therefore, to develop theories which go beyond words and show the living-out of the concepts. The meanings we give to our lives are in the actions we take as we try to live our values in our practices. The meanings of our values can be clarified in the course of their emergence and manifestation in practice.

So, in order to appreciate how we give meanings to our lives, we have to show in reality how we understand concepts such as education and learning by trying to live out those concepts. Dominant conceptual forms of theory, though a useful starting point, are insufficient by themselves. It is important as well to develop forms of theory which enable us to show the meanings we give to our lives through action. Actions speak louder than words.

I am on the side of Dewey and others who hold that education is a process which leads to learning for personal and social benefit. Like Dewey, I believe in the value of personal freedom and social justice, and the right of all people to live a peaceful and productive existence and enjoy loving relationships (Fromm, 1956). I encourage people to learn how they can improve whatever aspects of their practice they want to focus on; in action research terms this is often their own selves as they are in company with other selves.

On this view, action research is learning how to do things in more personally and socially beneficial ways, and education refers to the experience of the interaction between people which leads to further learning. As action researchers, we need to investigate the nature of the educative relationships we create, how we find ways of creating them, and how we can judge our own influence in the lives of others to ensure that we are influencing in directions of social good. We also need to find forms of representation that show adequately the meanings of our lives as we try to live our values in our practice.

Whose knowledge? Whose practice?

We are forever caught in politically constructed situations. Often our own selves are politically constructed: we give in to other people's expectations of how we should be rather than how we want to be.

Politics is highly visible in what counts as action research, what should be the focus of enquiry, whose practice is being studied by whom, and whose theory is valid. The situation is reminiscent of Sowell's description of what can happen when visions collide:

> One of the curious things about political opinions is how often the same people line up on opposite sides of different issues . . . A closer look at the arguments

on both sides often shows that they are reasoning from fundamentally different premises . . . They have different visions of how the world works.

(Sowell, 1987: 13)

They also have different visions of the value of people.

One vision of action research (which stems from a propositional worldview – see Chapter 2) says that one person may observe another and make judgements about their practice. This view assumes that ordinary people are not able to speak and act for themselves, and it dominates much contemporary thinking. Another vision (which stems from a dialectical worldview – see Chapter 2) is that all people, including 'ordinary' people, are capable of running their own lives and making judgements about the quality of their relationships with others. My own work is informed by ideas that equality is not only a matter of honouring the right of people to speak and act on their own behalf, but also of creating opportunities for them to do so.

These issues return us to the form of theory. If we believe people are able to think for themselves, we need to talk in a real-life way that respects their individuality and experience. Here is a story to illustrate the point.

I recently attended a workshop presented by a well-known educational researcher, who brought the audience through dynamic experiences which he then synthesised by means of an elegant five-point model to show us where we had come from and where we were now. During the presentation he had invited audience comment. I had wanted to make a point about the need always to situate personal enquiry within wider socio-political influences, but he did not allow me to speak, possibly because of time constraints, possibly not. At the end of the presentation when I was able to speak, I said that the issue I had wanted to raise had been well demonstrated through his presentation as well as his model. Conceptual models can be beautiful, and they work, provided we are obedient. If, however, as humans we choose to exercise our spontaneity and creativity we unfortunately step outside the designated boundaries. We do not conform to the model. We resist messages that this is how we should behave, and raise awkward questions and create tensions. Then we have to make decisions. Do we remain silent, and conform to beautiful but static models, and not risk upsetting important theorists, or do we act in the direction of our own values and challenge the oppressive nature of static conceptual models, and also possibly incur the wrath of powerful individuals and the groups they belong to? Where do we find spaces for the expression of our lives, and how do we safeguard those spaces from territorial invasion? These are all issues embedded in power and politics (and also money, as its possession determines issues of power and politics), and how secure we feel in our own sense of self to challenge or submit.

I am deeply concerned about the continuing dominance of abstract conceptual theory, about the unexamined assumptions in much of the literature that linguistic analyses of concepts such as education and action research are sufficient to address the questions 'What do we know?' and 'How do we come to know?' and that hypothesising about possible futures will enable us to address the question

'Knowledge for what?' Possible futures exist in the real present: it is what we do now that influences the future. We certainly need to integrate abstract theorising in the practical process of improving our actions, but we also need to generate theories from within the action to help us understand how we can exercise our choices to create ourselves as the kinds of persons we wish to be. Social change begins in people's minds as they make choices about which values to espouse and how to live in the direction of those values. Such choices are not easy, but they represent wondrous opportunities for personal and social development.

For you who are reading this book

This book is part of my own educational journey. My claim is that I am influencing people and the systems of knowledge they create in an educational way. I hope I encourage others to generate hope for personal and social renewal through their work, and help them find ways to turn the hope into reality.

This claim is part of my present best thinking. The thinking continues to develop, and whatever emerges, provided my journey continues to be educational, will in turn be the best for that moment. I hope it continues to do so, which will remind me always that I am alive before I die. The certainty of death throws into sharp relief the need to do something useful while the opportunity is here.

The theories I present here are developing, as the practice which generates them is developing. I hope the development is in the direction of social improvement. The theories are not presented as final statements, and they contain exciting dilemmas. I want to share the learning, both in terms of subjecting it to critical public scrutiny, and also in the hope that you will take what is useful and adopt or adapt it to your own context. Whatever your situation, if you are reading this you are aware of the centrality of learning for life itself, and how educative relationships can foster that learning. I hope the book provides an opportunity to strengthen our commitments to education.

Part I

What do we know?

The principles of action research

Reflecting on the experience of writing the first edition in 1988, I realise that I wrote about action research then as an object of enquiry and in an unproblematic way. Through reflection I have come to see the importance of critiquing and legitimating my claims through the problematics of practice. The opportunity to engage in action research in an intensified way came in the early 1990s when I began systematically supporting the professional learning of educators across the island of Ireland. This experience led me to get to grips with ideas about liberty, pluralism, power and legitimation processes.

My understanding of my work began to change. I began to see that my work was not only to provide routes to professional accreditation, but also to contribute to the thinking and practice of what I was beginning to understand as a good social order, a form of living in which people are free to make choices about creating their own identities and to recognise the need to negotiate those identities with others.

I began to see the link between action research and the creation of a good order; this link began to emerge because I was by then changing my understanding of the nature of action research. I came to see action research not as a set of concrete steps but as a process of learning from experience, a dialectical interplay between practice, reflection and learning. Working out ideas *is* the learning; working out how to live with one another *is* the peace process. A final outcome does not exist. We are always on the move. The life process in which we work out who we are and how we can live together successfully *is* the good social order.

Part 1 of this book sets out these ideas. It addresses issues of why I consistently view my practice as a research process, and spells out my aims and intentions in doing what I do, and broadly what I hope to achieve. It therefore gives the background and contexts of my research as I ask, 'How do I contribute to the development of a good social order through education?' I also test the validity of my provisional findings by drawing on theories in the literature, and these findings point in the direction of new research as I ask questions about the nature, acquisition and potential use value of educational knowledge.

1 What do we know?

The principles of action research

Action research is a name given to a particular way of researching your own learning. It is a practical way of looking at your practice in order to check whether it is as you feel it should be. If you feel that your practice is satisfactory you will be able to explain how and why you believe this is the case; you will be able to produce evidence to support your claims. If you feel that your practice needs attention in some way you will be able to take action to improve it, and then produce evidence to show in what way the practice has improved.

Because action research is done by you, the practitioner, it is often referred to as practitioner research, or a similar name such as practitioner-led or practitioner-based research. It is a form of research which can be undertaken by people in any context, regardless of their status or position. It involves you thinking carefully about what you are doing, so it can also be called a kind of self-reflective practice.

The idea of self-reflection is central. In traditional (empirical) forms of research researchers do research on other people. In action research researchers do research on themselves in company with other people, and those others are doing the same. No distinction is made between who is a researcher and who is a practitioner. Practitioners are potential researchers, and researchers are practitioners (some people who like to maintain their status as 'pure' researchers do not always see it this way, though). Traditional researchers enquire into other people's lives and speak about other people as data. Action researchers enquire into their own lives and speak with other people as colleagues. Action research is an enquiry by the self into the self, undertaken in company with others acting as research participants and critical learning partners.

Action research involves learning in and through action and reflection, and it is conducted in a variety of contexts, including the social and caring sciences, education, organisation and administration studies, and management. Because action research is always to do with learning, and learning is to do with education and growth, many people regard it as a form of educational research.

In one sense, there is no such 'thing' as action research. It is important always to remember this. Sometimes people write about action research as if it were a self-contained object of enquiry, existing separate from themselves. I am doing so now. On this view, action research can become an abstract discipline, a set of procedures which can be applied to practice. It can then turn from being a living process to a linguistic abstraction, and this tends to distort the values of justice and individual autonomy which animate action research. It is important always to locate discussions about action research within the real-life experience of real-life people. The 'meaning' of action research is in the way people live together.

While there might be no such thing as action research, there are people who are action researchers. They might not call themselves by that name, but if they wished to give their work a theoretical framework, they could well call the framework action research. When people first encounter the idea of action research they often say, 'This is what I do in any case, only now there is an organising framework for it.' The idea of action research refers to the theoretical framework which guides practice. Action research is not a thing in itself; the term always implies a process of people interacting with one another.

Action researchers share certain sets of beliefs, commitments and hopes. What they do (action research) is a set of practices which demonstrates those beliefs, commitments and hopes in practice. They undertake research to help them learn how to create social hope (Rorty, 1999) and to take action to try to realise the hope in terms of social evolution.

Questions arise, therefore, about what action researchers do, and how and why they do it, questions to do with how we view ourselves (ontology), how we come to know (epistemology), how we do things (methodology), and what we hope to achieve (socio-political intent). These aspects are always interrelated.

Aspects of research

Action research (for that matter all kinds of research) is more than just doing activities. It is a form of practice which involves data gathering, reflection on the action as it is presented through the data, generating evidence from the data, and making claims to knowledge based on conclusions drawn from validated evidence. When we come to producing reports, it is not enough only to offer descriptions and activities lists. Explanations need to be given for the activities, in terms of the researcher's values, intentions and purposes for doing the research. For example, if a researcher makes a claim that they have helped others become more confident, the values that inform their work include the idea that people should feel respected. So when people do demonstrate their confidence, such as asking a question in public, the researcher could claim that they had fulfilled their values, and that they had influenced the quality of someone's life for good.

It is helpful to be familiar with some key ideas and terms used in educational research.

Research is generally held to involve the following:

*   *ontology* – the way we view ourselves, a theory of being
*   *epistemology* – how we understand knowledge, including how knowledge is acquired
*   *methodology* – how we do things.

Educational research also involves issues of politics, because it is always socially embedded; it is done by real people with the intent of illuminating, explaining and improving human interaction in education settings. Action research has as a main purpose the generation of knowledge which leads to improvement of understanding and experience for social benefit.

DOING ACTION RESEARCH

What do action researchers believe in? Ontological issues

Action researchers believe that people are able to create their own identities and allow other people to create theirs. They try to find ways of accommodating multiple values perspectives. This is surely very difficult when one set of values is radically at odds with another. They try to find ways to live together in spite of their potential differences. Living together successfully requires hard work and considerable effort to understand the other's point of view; this means developing their potentials to care, and recognising and suspending their own prejudices.

Creating the kind of societies they feel are good societies involves their personal commitment to action. This means having the courage to speak and act in ways which are often contested. They hold a vision of a future which is better than the present, characterised by creative, life-affirming ways of living. The future is embodied in the present; they can realise future potentialities by improving what they are doing in relation with others in the present. They know that if they abandon the vision of a better society in the light of the troubles of the present one, they will probably settle into stasis. However, if they try to do something, just one positive life-enhancing action, there is hope. Improvement is still improvement, no matter how small.

Action researchers accept the responsibility of ensuring that their own lives are in order before they make judgements about other people's. This means honestly critiquing their practice, recognising what is good and building on strengths, as well as understanding what needs attention and taking action to improve it. It involves commitment to the idea that learning will transform into purposeful personal action for social benefit.

They often express these ontological assumptions in the language of values. Action research rests on ideas to do with truth, social justice, compassionate ways of living, respect for pluralistic forms. Often action researchers live in social contexts where these values are prized in principle but denied in practice. The realities of their contexts often show preference for privileged elites rather than the underprivileged and marginalised. Action researchers aim to understand these issues in order to change present realities into futures which are more in tune with their values.

How do action researchers come to know? Epistemological issues

Epistemology is the name given to the study of what we know and how we come to know it. Traditional views of scientific enquiry tend to see knowledge as a free-standing unit, with an existence of its own, residing 'out there' in books and databases. In this view knowledge is divorced from the people who create it.

Action researchers see knowledge as something they do, a living process. People can generate their own knowledge from their experience of living and learning. Knowledge is never static or complete; it is in a constant process of development as new understandings emerge. This view of knowledge regards reality as a process of evolution, surprising and unpredictable. There are no fixed answers, because answers would immediately become obsolete in a constantly changing future. The very idea of answer becomes meaningless; answers transform into new questions. Life is a process of asking questions to reveal new potentialities. Action researchers ask questions of the kind, 'I wonder what would happen if . . .?' They aim to disturb fixed systems of knowing rather than maintain them.

Learning in this view is rooted in experience. It involves reflecting on the experience of practice (a process of critical discernment), deciding whether the practice was in line with your espoused values base, and then deciding on future action as a result of the reflection. If you consider practice good, how can you develop it to deal with an uncertain future? If you consider it less than good, how can you improve it?

Some theorists believe that learning happens only in critical episodes. Certainly it does, but learning also happens all the time, in our moment-to-moment living. We learn how to walk, to catch a ball, to avoid trouble, to respond to our feelings. Learning, says Mary Catherine Bateson (1994), often happens peripherally; we learn a good deal without effort and without conscious intent. Learning can be accelerated and intensified through critical awareness, and reinforced through intellectual study. Learning mainly involves making new connections and reconfiguring present knowledge in terms of its potential use value, and this process is often carried out at a level not accessible to conscious awareness.

How do action researchers act? Methodological issues

Action researchers regard learning and experience as processes which enable individuals to make choices about who they are and how they are together. However, people's choices often conflict, so they have to be negotiated and accommodated. This can be very difficult, but it can be done if people try to see one another's point of view. The methodology of action research is that people ask questions such as 'How do I do this better? How do we understand?' They do not aim for consensus or harmony, but they do try to create spaces of tolerance to negotiate differences.

This can happen because reflection on action is an inherent part of an action research methodology. The idea of reflective practice was originally popularised by Donald Schön (1983). Reflection on action makes sense, however, only when practice is seen as in relation with others, a process of dialogue and encounter (Bryk *et al.*, 1993). For some, myself included, the ideas of encounter, connectedness and relationship can be understood as a form of spirituality. Capra *et al.* (1992), for example, believe that relation should be understood as belonging. We arc all connected in deep ways, and, because we are made of the same stuff as stars

(Feynman, 1999), we are also connected to the whole of creation. We belong to one another and ultimately to the universe.

These views have implications for how people understand their practice. In traditional epistemologies, practice tends to be seen as something separate from practitioners. People might imagine work as in a building or an office, for example. I used to think like this; I regarded work as a thing I did. On a relational view, work and practice are how we are in relationship with other people. The focus of the work is how to nurture creative and life-giving encounters. Action researchers regard their work as ensuring that encounters with others are opportunities for learning and growth. When they reflect on practice they are reflecting on their relationships with others, and whether those others have benefited from the encounter. This can be a major test for judging the quality of the practice: has the other person benefited from the encounter? The implications are awesome. If we are always in relation and those relationships have potential influence for changing people's lives, even in small ways, how great is the responsibility to ensure that the influence is life-affirming. If we make ourselves who we are through our capacity for choosing, how important it is that we choose to avoid doing harm.

What are the socio-political implications of our knowledge?

There are serious implications in these views. Here are some of them.

Challenging dominant epistemologies

The purpose of research is generally understood as gathering data and testing it in order to generate new knowledge which can produce new theories of how reality works. In traditional views theories exist as an abstract body of knowledge which informs practice, a theory-into-practice model. In traditional education settings, whether in formal schooling or professional education, there is an expectation that people will attend lessons and take notes, but not raise questions. Some researchers (see Chapter 3) produce conceptual models which work in practice provided people are obedient and comply with how the model says they ought to behave. If people exercise their independence of mind and spirit, however, and disagree with the model itself or the fact that they are supposed to agree with abstract theory, they are often seen as disruptive and anarchic.

The traditional positivist view of research and theory has dominated Western institutional thinking and practice for centuries. New movements such as action research have challenged traditional views. Such challenges are naturally unwelcome to dominant elites, who then gather force to put down the insurgence. They use a range of control strategies including ridicule and marginalisation, what Lyotard (1984) calls intellectual terrorism. The most characteristic response is to pretend that critique does not exist. When a critical mass builds up, however, sufficient to show that it does, other measures must be exercised. The most characteristic of these is to use the language of 'radical', 'unorthodox' and 'alternative'. There is nothing radical or unorthodox about people wanting to have a say in their own lives. It is important not to let propaganda or fear of being labelled reactionary stand in the way of realising one's vision for what could be a better way of life.

The issue then becomes the legitimacy of forms of theory, who is entitled to generate theory, and how the theory is judged – 'who decides what knowledge is, and who knows what needs to be decided' (Lyotard, 1984: 9). Ball (1990: 17), drawing on the work of Michel Foucault, says that it is not only about 'what can be said and thought but also about who can speak, when, where and with what authority. Discourses embody meaning and social relationship; they constitute both subjectivity and power relations.' The issue then extends to not only what should be judged a worthwhile theory but also who should be judged a worthwhile person.

The topology of epistemological landscapes

Schön (1983, 1995) speaks of the topology of professional landscapes and their characteristic epistemologies. There is a high ground, he says, which favours technical rationality (what I have so far called propositional forms of knowledge), and a swampy lowlands which values intuitive, practical forms. The high ground tends to be found in institutions and is peopled mainly by elitist intelligentsias from the corporate and formal education worlds. Chomsky has often referred to these as a 'high priesthood'. The high priesthood is much occupied with generating abstract theories about issues which, while valuable in themselves, often have little to do with important aspects of everyday living. Because of the prestigious social positioning of the theorists, their abstract form of theory has come to be seen as dominant. Practitioners, on the other hand, deal with issues of everyday significance, but, because practitioners are not viewed as legitimate knowers, either by the high priesthood or by themselves (because 'ordinary' people are systematically taught to devalue their own contributions), their form of theory tends to be regarded as practical problem-solving rather than proper research.

The situation is topsy-turvy to the realities of daily living. Precisely those issues of daily significance which occupy practitioners are trivialised, along with the status of the practitioners as knowledge workers and theory generators, while abstract theorising continues to maintain institutional legitimacy.

Schön calls for a reappraisal of what counts as scholarship. Research which addresses the important issues of daily living needs to be given as much prestige as traditional scholarship. Practical theorising is an important methodology for making holistic cultural, social and intellectual progress. Practical, experiential theorists should have status equal to abstract theorists in corporate and higher education contexts: they are in the front line of social theorising. Practical forms of theory are as legitimate as 'pure' conceptual forms. The most powerful and appropriate form of theory for dealing with contemporary social issues is one which is located in, and generated out of, practice, and which values tacit knowledge as much as cognitive knowledge. This all comes down to action research, a way of researching one's own practice and generating personal theories of practice which show the process of self-monitoring, evaluation of practice, and purposeful action to improve the practice for social benefit.

Levels of adequacy

In 1965, and focusing on linguistic analysis, Noam Chomsky explained that research can operate at three levels of adequacy: observational, descriptive and explanatory. In a sense, all research begins with observation, and most research offers descriptions of events. In 1960s linguistics the dominant research methodology was behaviouristic. The aim was to study a particular language, gather instances of its significant features, and provide descriptions of the language under study (Lyons, 1970). The same tendency is visible today across the social sciences, education research and organisation study. Everywhere there are descriptions of how things work, or ought to work, and what needs to be done to make them work in this way. These are inert theoretical models. They work in principle, but often there is no live evidence to show that they work in practice.

It is not enough, in Schön's view, to stay at the level of hypothetical theorising. It is necessary to move to explanation in Chomsky's sense. Moving from observation and description of action means moving to offering explanations for action. The focus of research then develops from observing and describing what is happening to considering why it is happening – that is, the reasons and intentions of the person which inform the behaviour.

The issue remains, however, whose research is it? Some views of action research say it is acceptable for an external researcher to observe, describe and explain the actions of others who are doing action research. This belief animates an interpretive view of action research (see Chapter 3). In my opinion, this is a distortion of the values of democracy and respect for others who should be regarded as thinking people who have the capacity to judge their own practice, also recognising that the process of self-evaluation is likely to be enhanced within a community of critical friends. For action research to operate successfully as a methodology for social change, the locus of responsibility for conducting the research needs to shift from an 'external' researcher who is observing and describing other people's activities to practitioners themselves who give accounts of their own activities in terms of their values and hopes.

E-theories and I-theories

I again draw on the work of Chomsky to support this view.

In his *Knowledge of Language* (1986) Chomsky developed the idea of E-language and I-language. The emphasis in traditional American linguistics in the 1970s and 1980s was still on the sound and word structure of sentences, and a language could be understood 'as a collection (or system) of actions or behaviours of some sort' (p. 20). Chomsky refers to this as an 'externalized language' (E-language). An 'internalized language' (I-language), on the other hand, is 'some element of the mind of the person who knows the language acquired by the learner, and used by the speaker-hearer' (p. 22). In 2000 Chomsky developed the concept of I-conceptual and I-belief systems, a concept that revolves around the internalised nature of beliefs and ideas. This indicates a shift away from description of language or thinking or theory generation, as an external object of study, towards an explanation of how language or thinking or theory generation informs the way a person creates their own version of reality.

This is a most important concept, and I wish to develop the notion of 'E' and 'I' (as I have already done in McNiff 1993) to refer to different forms of theory and ways of coming to know. An E-theory exists as a form of theory external to its creator and which is generated from study of the properties of external objects. This is a propositional form of theory, much admired in social scientific analysis, behaviourist in orientation, and synchronic (in linguistics this is understood as abstracted from time). An I-theory is a dialectical form of theory, a property of an individual's belief system, and is diachronic (in linguistics this is understood as oriented in real time). This view is helpful for understanding different forms of theory, not only for linguistics but also for broad areas of human enquiry, including educational research. In this book I take the view that action research leads to the generation of I-theories of knowledge, theories which are already located within the practitioner's tacit forms of knowing, and which emerge in practice as personal forms of acting and knowing. These theories are linked with other I-belief systems – values, for example. The way the theories manifest as living practices is congruent with the belief systems of the knower.

Debates like this, to do with how we understand the process of research and the generation of theory, however, give rise to struggles about the nature and practice of action research – what it is and who owns it (or, when action research is taken as a term denoting people in company with one another, who we are and who creates our identities).

The struggle for action research as a living practice

At the moment three distinct developmental trends are visible in the literature of action research: an interpretive, a critical theoretic and a living theory approach (see Chapter 3). Interpretive and critical theoretic approaches clearly work at the levels of observation and description: while they also offer explanations for practice, these explanations are offered within sets of propositional relationships. It also seems that many people offering action research courses in higher- and formal-education contexts tend to operate within interpretive and critical theoretic rather than living theory frameworks. It is less problematic to observe other people doing action research than to do it oneself.

Engaging with living theory approaches means, as Whitehead says, placing the 'living I' at the centre of our enquiries and recognising ourselves potentially as living contradictions. We might believe we are working in an effective and morally committed manner and then find from our own self-evaluation that we are denying much of what we believe in.

Here is an example from the doctoral work of Caroline Clarke as she speaks about trying to live out her values of care. Outlining her research (Clarke, 2000: 1–2), she says:

> My study focuses on two main areas: my personal and professional journey as an educator and my attempt to change and influence the culture of my school

with regard to discipline . . . I describe the 'epiphanies' that brought me to realise that I was outside my 'value world' and consequently experiencing a drain on my emotional and spiritual energy as a result of my workplace role. Following these realisations I began searching not only for answers but also for understanding of what was happening to me in those moments where my values were compromised and I became what Jack Whitehead (1989) describes as a 'living contradiction'. The answers came in the form of reading, observation and action on reflection, and the solution came in the form of change. The change was two-fold, in me and in the wider educational system of which I was a part. My diary of the time (June, 2000) reads: 'To hope for a change is essential but it takes courage to go beyond hope and bring about change. It must be the kind of courage which not only seeks to change oneself, but also the circumstances and people around you, despite the opposition.'

Self-study is now widely recognised as a powerful influence for personal and social renewal (see the foreword by Douglas Barnes, in Hamilton, 1998; Zeichner, 1999). It does mean accepting the responsibility of accounting for our own practice, and, in work contexts, accounting for our own professionalism. We offer descriptions and explanations for our work by producing professional narratives to show that the work did impact beneficially on others. We gather and test data of our practice and produce evidence to show that our claims are well founded. Those with whom we work state that they have benefited (or not as the case may be), and those with whom they are working testify that they in turn are benefiting (or not) (see, for example, Delong, 2000; Lillis, 2000b). So it is possible to trace lines of influence from ourselves to others with whom we might have no personal contact, but whose lives we can claim to have touched. There are, says Bakhtin (1986), voices in everything. I am alone as I write, but I am influenced by the voices in the texts I have read and the seminars I have attended, as well as the voices in the supermarket and at the airport. You are listening to my voice as you read, and responding, and in turn others will hear your voice and be stirred. How can we ensure that we are speaking well, and using our influence for others' benefit? In some instances the lines of influence are too complex and it is impossible to know the extent of our influence. An implication is that, in all the contexts of our lives, whether its effects are visible or not, we need to ensure that our influence leads to life-enhancing growth for all.

Descriptive E-approaches cannot do this. They work from a behaviourist orientation in which an external researcher offers accounts of other people's action. In this view, as McNamara and O'Hara (2000) and Zuber-Skerritt (1996) rightly say, it is difficult to show how action research can influence organisational growth or collective action. The process of influencing social change begins with the process of personal change: 'change can only come about when the individuals who belong to a particular organization can see the point in changing' (Rizvi, 1989: 227). It is pointless to produce abstract models of social change and expect other people to apply them to their own circumstances or locate themselves within the models (as, for example, Zuber-Skerritt does in 1992a and 1996). Bourdieu's (1990) idea about the reality of the model being more powerful than the model of reality becomes very real.

I am not saying that observations and descriptions are unimportant. They are important, but they do not go far enough. It is not enough for an external observer to describe another person's actions and then to present an account of those actions as if to give a full explanation of their reality. The practice is also ethically questionable. I am saying that, while observation and description are essential first steps, it is important to go beyond and offer explanations. Explanations are the I-theories people generate to show their own process of learning and development. Moving on like this is a generative transformational process in which present forms transform into increasingly robust forms; observations turn into descriptions which turn into explanations. The whole developmental process is integrated within the life of the person who is telling the story. An approach which might be deemed educational would perhaps be to place evidence from living theory accounts alongside the propositional theories generated from spectator research, and so show the enhanced validity of those living theories which explain the practices and learning of individuals.

Action research for explanatory adequacy

Here is an example of how descriptions can turn into explanations, how propositional theory can turn into real-world action. The example is taken from the action research literature about the nature of action research.

There are many well-known descriptions of action research. Here are two of the most famous.

Description 1

Action research is a form of *collective* self-reflective enquiry undertaken by participants in social situations in order to improve the rationality and justice of their own social or educational practices, as well as their understanding of these practices and the situations in which these practices are carried out.

(Kemmis and McTaggart, 1988: 5; emphasis in original)

Description 2

If yours is a situation in which

- people reflect and improve (or develop) their own work and their own situations
- by tightly interlinking their reflection and action
- and also making their experience public not only to other participants but also to other persons interested in and concerned about the work and the situations (i.e. their (public) theories and practices of the work and the situation)

and if yours is a situation in which there is increasingly

- data-gathering by participants themselves (or with the help of others) in relation to their own questions
- participation (in problem-posing and in answering questions) in decision-making
- power-sharing and the relative suspension of hierarchical ways of working towards industrial democracy
- collaboration among members of the group as a 'critical community'
- self-reflection, self-evaluation and self-management by autonomous and responsible persons and groups
- learning progressively (and publicly) by doing and by making mistakes in a 'self reflective spiral' of planning, acting, observing, reflecting, replanning, etc.
- reflection which supports the idea of the (self-) reflective practitioner

then yours is a situation in which *action research* is occurring.
(inclusive working definition drawn up collaboratively at the International Symposium on Action Research, Brisbane, March 1989, and reproduced in Zuber-Skerritt, 1992b: 14; emphasis in original)

So far, these are linguistic descriptions of action research. However, some of the authors go on to show how they turn their linguistic descriptions into real-life explanations (see Atweh *et al.*, 1998); they show how they lived out the principles they spell out. More of such accounts are needed.

Future directions in action research

These issues are important for future developments. Action researchers need to show their collective intent to live out the values which inform their work. Because they write about action research they inevitably position themselves as action researchers, so they need to take care that they do not stay at the level of abstract analysis. If they write about practice but do not explain their own they are not engaging with the issues they are speaking about. Contradictory situations arise. The contradictions are methodological, in the same way as when we try to teach people how to swim on dry land; and also ethical, as when we talk at people about the value of dialogue. Action researchers cannot afford to be armchair philosophers if they wish to maintain their professional and ethical integrity. Action research means action, not by some, but by all, but this means honesty and courage, and is not easy for those positioned as members of intelligentsias. We are all judged by our actions, especially when action is part of our trade mark. We all make our own decisions about these things.

So what do we know?

The community of educational action researchers knows a great deal about the procedures and principles of action research. We do not know so much about how action research can be used as a form of living practice in the evolution of good social orders, although a good deal of work has appeared recently in this regard. Jack Whitehead, Pam Lomax, I and others have supported the development of networks of practitioners who have produced accounts of educational development, and who in turn support others to produce accounts of how they do the same. The support of this networking is managed in a non-hierarchical, non-coercive way. It is a question of educational influence, a dialogue of equals. We constitute educational communities who are hoping to transform themselves through learning for social benefit.

I like Lynn Davies's (1990: 210) view of the management of learning communities: 'to achieve equity and efficiency, out go coercion, streaming, hierarchies and leadership, and in come federalism, power-sharing, organizational responsiveness'. This view is shown in our educational networks. Impressive bodies of validated case studies now exist in the Universities of Bath, Kingston and the West of England in the UK; in Brock and Nipissing in Canada; in Limerick in Ireland. These case studies constitute a major body of educational research literature. The influence of practitioners' ideas is being felt in their contexts of practice (for example, Delong, 2000; Evans, 1996; Lomax, 1996; McNiff *et al.*, 2000).

Action research has been legitimated by the Academy as a powerful and valid form of learning. The task is now to extend the range of influence. While it is not too difficult to show influence within supportive communities (see Chapters 5 and 9–12), it is more problematic when it is a question of influencing others who are indifferent or hostile, or whose interests are to do with careerism and profit-making rather than education. How the knowledge can be disseminated, and the influence intensified, is discussed in Chapter 4.

I will now move on to consider the relationships between theory and practice.

2   How do we come to know?

Linking theory and practice

This chapter deals with issues about how knowledge is generated and its relationship with practice.

Educational research is socially and politically embedded. It is always undertaken by a real person or persons, within a particular context, for a designated purpose. Research does not just happen. It is planned to greater or lesser degrees, and has an overall design for what it hopes to show (a claim to knowledge), how it is going to gather and present data in support of the claim to knowledge, and how it is going to show the validity of the claim through some kind of legitimation process. Research aims to create new knowledge and gather data, and to test and generate new theories that are more appropriate for human living than previous theories. As soon as issues such as 'new knowledge' and 'more appropriate theories' surface, however, politics becomes prominent, because what counts as knowledge and theory is often contested by different theorists working in their particular contexts and with their own agendas. Research and theory generation involve tightly interlinked areas of influence, social purpose, justice, power, politics and personal identity. When speaking about educational research it is important to locate the conversation in historical, cultural and socio-political contexts.

Here, therefore, I wish to outline some of the main aspects that have led to the emergence of the action research movement, and suggest why the work is often hotly contested, and why, for me and others, a main task is to investigate what might be the form of logic (way of thinking) most appropriate for describing and explaining action enquiries.

The chapter is organised as three sections. First, I will outline some well-established typologies of knowledge, human interests and research. Second, I hope to show the development of action research within these typologies. Third, I will suggest ways in which the areas could be developed in terms of what Schön (1995) identifies as the new scholarship.

TYPOLOGIES OF KNOWLEDGE, HUMAN INTERESTS AND RESEARCH

Typologies of knowledge

There are different kinds of knowledge and different ways of knowing. It is widely held that there are three main kinds of knowledge – know that, know how and personal knowledge; and two main systems of knowing, or forms of logic, by which knowledge is acquired and expressed – propositional and dialectical.

Forms of knowledge

Know that, also called propositional and technical rational knowledge, refers to knowledge about facts and figures. Knowledge exists 'out there', external to a knower. It is an abstract body of information about the world which is found in books and other retrieval systems. Knowledge is often seen as a commodity to be acquired, moved around and exchanged for other goods. This is particularly so for post-industrial 'knowledge-creating' societies: 'Knowledge is and will be produced in order to be sold' (Lyotard, 1984: 4). The fixed body of knowledge holds truths about the way things are. When people claim, 'I know that x,' they can produce evidence to support the claim by referring to external sources. Know that is linked with the idea of E-theories, and refers to bodies of public knowledge which are external to the knower.

  Know how, also called procedural knowledge, refers to procedures and also capabilities. Know how is not a fixed body of knowledge external to ourselves, but involves practical knowing. 'I know how to do this' refers to a way of acting in the world, and the claim to knowledge can be supported by demonstrating, for example, that one can ride a bike or do mathematics. On this view, know how is often linked with skills and competencies, though knowing how to do something does not guarantee that one can do it. Ryle (1949) contains an account of know that and know how.

  Personal knowledge, also called tacit knowledge (Polanyi, 1958, 1967), refers to a subjective way of knowing that often cannot be rationalised. Often we cannot articulate what we know; we 'just know'. It seems that we all have a vast fund of tacit knowledge, possibly gleaned from experience, possibly part of our genetic inheritance, that enables us to act in particular ways without recourse to external facts or authority. Personal knowledge is linked with the idea of I-theories, and refers to the latent knowledge which is within the individual's mind–brain.

Ways of knowing (forms of logic)

In speaking about ways of knowing, it is common to identify two major epistemological traditions: propositional (or formal) and dialectical.

  Propositional (or formal) logic refers to abstract ways of knowing. We view reality and knowledge as external objects; we study them and make proposals about how they work. This is a conceptual system of knowing which uses an abstract form of logic; it regards theories as static models of reality which may be understood intellectually. When we think and express our knowledge in propositional ways, we make positive statements about the way we think about things. Abstract forms *abstract* from reality; the thinking is abstract, a conceptual exercise. This form of logic, often associated with Aristotle, who wanted to eliminate contradiction from rational thought, is much valued by the Western intellectual tradition and informs most of its social, particularly institutional, practices.

Dialectical logic refers to fluid, relational forms of knowing. We view reality as something we are part of. Knowing is a process of creating new forms out of previous ones, a process of becoming. It is a to-and-fro, ebb-and-flow process in which one thing transforms into another. Dialectics often takes the form of question and answer, where one answer generates a new question, so nothing is ever complete or final. This way of knowing is embodied in the knower and their practice. It is embodied, not abstract; real life, not conceptual. This view is part of an ancient tradition, often associated with but existing long before Plato, who saw contradiction as part of life processes, the need to hold the one and the many together at the same time, and it is at the heart of many non-Western ways of knowing.

Typologies of human interests

Habermas (1972, 1974), a major theorist in social science, rejected the view that knowledge generation is a neutral activity done by an external 'mind' somewhere, resulting in the production of 'pure' knowledge. Instead he suggested that knowledge is an activity undertaken by a real person who is driven by particular desires and interests. In this view, knowledge is always constituted of human interests. Habermas categorised personal–social practices in terms of three broad sets of interests: the technical, the practical and the emancipatory.

Technical interests are mainly concerned with controlling the environment through the production of technical rational knowledge. The aim of knowledge is to support technical and scientific progress. Although this has come to be the dominant epistemology in technologised societies, it is a quite narrow view which sees knowledge as instrumental activity which can be measured quantitatively and precisely. Technical rationality is generally seen as the form of knowledge most appropriate for contemporary social and work practices. This book does not hold this view, suggesting that other forms of knowledge are also essential for human living.

Practical interests focus on understanding, meaning-making and interpretation. Habermas maintains that communicative action goes beyond rational interaction and scientific enquiry, and involves understanding other people and their lifeworlds. Communicative action aims to generate intersubjective agreement, where people come together to share their ideas and work towards agreement, even when this is possibly agreement within disagreement. This process, however, can distort the understandings we arrive at, for what we do and think are always subject to wider historical and cultural influences of which we may or may not be aware. It is important, says Habermas, to understand those forces and find ways of dealing with them.

Emancipatory interests help us to free ourselves from dominating forces which control our knowledge and actions. We learn how to recognise and deal with influences which try to force us to become the people others wish us to be, and we work consistently to create our own identities. We recognise the politically constituted nature of all our social practices, and work within those frameworks to liberate our own thinking in order to take more purposeful action in shaping our lives.

Typologies of research

Arising out of Habermas's work, which itself arose out of an investigation of the nature of knowledge and its acquisition, a three-paradigm approach has come to be widely accepted today (for detailed commentaries see Bassey, 1999; Carr and Kemmis, 1986; Ernest, 1994; Hitchcock and Hughes, 1995; McNiff, 2000). In research contexts, a paradigm (as the idea has been adapted from Kuhn, 1970) is understood as a set of ideas and approaches, mental models which influence the development of particular intellectual and social frameworks. The main research paradigms are the empirical, the interpretive and the critical theoretic, and these reflect the categories of technical, practical and emancipatory interests. These paradigms in turn may contain their own sub-sets.

Empirical research

Empirical research is rooted in the Newtonian–Cartesian worldview. In this view the natural world can be understood as a set of interrelated parts, and one part causes certain effects in others. Phenomena are often seen as pieces of machinery, which act in a predetermined way, with predeterminable outcomes (see, for example, Davies, 1992). Descartes said that the mind and body were separate entities. This view gave rise to a philosophy of dualism: that is, things could be understood in terms of binary opposites: either – or, not both – and. The worldview was one of fragmentation, isolation and alienation (Dawkins, 1987). In historical accounts of research the idea of 'empirical' as an objective methodology often changes to 'empiricist', with overtones of control and domination, particularly when the metaphors of the natural sciences are transferred to human activity. People are studied as objects. Like machine parts, they occupy particular places which they should keep to maintain the equilibrium of an established order.

Early empiricists believed that only objects 'out there' were worthy of study. Anything which could not be seen, heard, felt, smelt or tasted was not real, so 'imaginary' phenomena such as hopes and intentions should not be taken seriously. Studying reality involved a careful process of experimentation, usually involving control and experimental groups. The aim was to show how variables could be manipulated to predict and control behaviour in terms of cause and effect; data generated was subject to quantitative analysis.

This view travelled extensively throughout human enquiry and is still highly regarded. Traditional forms of education and education research take a cause-and-effect view: 'if x then y' (see Bassey, 1999). The same applies to many work practices; management, for example, is often seen as controlling people in order to produce certain outcomes.

The validity of empirical research is still judged in terms of replicability and generalisability. If an experiment were repeated in a new situation, would it follow a specified method exactly, and could its results be generalised to other situations? If these two criteria are not met, the research and its theory might be rejected as invalid.

Critique

When applied to social settings, the machine analogy breaks down. It works provided people are prepared to behave in ways which are approved by more powerful knowers. When people challenge power relationships, however, and act in ways of their own choosing, conflict frequently arises.

In traditional empirical approaches learning is managed by means of a model of instruction. People are expected to receive information and apply it to their work. The locus of power is in the external researcher who gathers data about the situation. People become data to be manipulated and spoken about. Boundaries are established as to what can and cannot be done. The values base of human living is systematically factored out. Participants are discouraged from acting as agents and are required rather to become skilled technicians who apply received knowledge.

The epistemological basis of empirical approaches is that theory determines practice. Practitioners are encouraged to fit their practice into a given theory, not to question, and not to exercise their own independence of mind and action, a situation which entirely denies the creativity and spontaneity of educational practice or the self-reflective nature of responsible action. Knowledge is seen as a thing; in the market orientation of many contemporary education philosophies, knowledge is not a process to be engaged in but a commodity to be acquired and sold (see above, p. 28; see also Winter, 1999).

The commodification of education and its management disregards questions of the kind 'How do I improve my practice?' (Whitehead, 1989). This kind of question sees the knowledge base of practice as fluid, developmental, generative and transformational; all people are potential knowers who create their own answers to practice as they investigate it, and so generate their own personal theories of learning, teaching and management from within that practice. Education is a creative process which is based on caring relationships. The epistemology of practice is one of spontaneity and generativity, a knowledge base which can lead to educative, life-enhancing encounters.

Interpretive research

In empirical approaches participants are data whose personal involvement is factored out; any personal intervention by them would contaminate and potentially skew the results. The interpretive approach, however, acknowledges the existence of practitioners as real-life participants in the research. In some views their accounts are as valid as those of the researcher–observer's.

The interpretive tradition mainly grew out of sociological enquiry, as the social sciences began to dislodge a worldview of human action as deterministic. It arose initially out of the hermeneutic tradition, the name given to the practice of the interpretation of religious texts by Protestant theologians in the seventeenth century (see Carr and Kemmis, 1986), and which later came to be associated with literature and the arts. From the nineteenth century onwards more efficient communications and travel opportunities gave rise to an interest in anthropological and naturalistic research: researchers began to study people in their own settings. A number of perspectives developed including phenomenology and ethnomethodology (see McNiff, 2000), and debates arose within the movement as to whose voices should be heard – the researcher's or the researchees'. The same dilemma as that found in empiricist approaches came to prominence: who had control of the research process and whose theory was being generated? While interpretive research valued the importance of people as actors, the question still remained as to who was writing the script.

During the 1960s and 1970s a type of ethnographic research arose in education studies which was known, among other terms, as illuminative evaluation (Parlett and Hamilton, 1976). This gradually evolved as case-study research (see Bassey, 1999), and its underpinning ideologies included that of democratic popular involvement in the research process and the interpretation of its findings. This view, however, is frequently distorted in much case-study research, where the external 'outsider' researcher does research on an insider's practices, reflecting a view critiqued by commentators such as James (1991) and Chomsky (1996) that ordinary people are often believed incapable of speaking for themselves. This view tends to be perpetuated by elites who like to keep things that way.

Case-study research has become a major approach in much social scientific and education enquiry. Its methodologies involve systematic collection of objective data, and rigorous analysis to arrive at agreed interpretations of the data. A main technique to ensure analytical rigour is triangulation. The Open University course definition of triangulation is:

> cross-checking the existence of certain phenomena and the veracity of individual accounts by gathering data from a number of informants and a number of sources and subsequently comparing and contrasting one account with another in order to produce as full and balanced a study as possible.
> (OU course E811 Study Guide, 1988: 54, cited in Bell, 1993: 64)

Depending on the commitments of the researcher, the data and its interpretation may or may not be made available to participants for their scrutiny and possible reinterpretation.

Critique

This view of the research process and the positioning of the researcher and research participants is potentially little different from that of traditional empirical research. The same power relationships exist as to who is regarded as a legitimate knower, whose practice is to be studied, and whose knowledge counts. The external researcher is entitled to regard people as objects of study, and to make statements about their actions and the purposes and intentions that inform those actions. The external researcher speaks on behalf of other people. The form of theory remains conceptual: the researcher generates a theory about an external situation.

When this situation is applied to action research, as it frequently is, the contradictions are clear. On the one hand, researchers produce high-sounding rhetoric about democracy and the rights of people to be involved in decision-making, and on the other hand systematically rule people out of the decision-making process of the research. There is a clear assumption that it is acceptable for researchers to watch other people doing their action research, to advise on what they should do and how they should act. The contradictions exist in the continuation of a power relationship that positions the researcher as external to the situation, but still able to interpret the situation and make judgements about other people; and also in the fact that the researcher advises other people what to do without necessarily taking their own advice. I wonder whether they see this need. In my view, those positioned as appointed researchers should engage in the same process of critical discernment and informed action which they advise other people to engage in, and take their own advice. Perhaps, however, it is a significant feature of many in authority that they do not see the need to change, and will not change without a challenge (Douglas, cited by Chomsky, 1996). It would appear that some interpretive views rest on a limited conception of democracy and participation (Ball, 1987): for some people, models of democracy are to be applied, rather than lived, a process of convenient discrimination rather than moral commitment.

Critical theoretic research

A new swell of critical voices began to be heard from the 1930s onwards. The most coherent were heard from what later came to be known as the Frankfurt School (Horkheimer, Adorno, Marcuse and later Habermas), who said that then current methodologies were inadequate for social scientific enquiry because they failed to recognise the historical, cultural and social situatedness of researchers. People could not comment on their experience unless they understood how that experience was shaped by their own situatedness. They could not be free until they realised they were unfree.

A new approach was needed which enabled people to become aware of the historical and cultural forces which had influenced them and their situations. People needed to understand the power-constituted nature of their lives, and learn how to challenge. This view constituted an ideology critique which enabled people to become aware of their historical and cultural conditioning and find ways to recreate their personal and social realities.

Critical theory developed as a systematic approach to offer both an oppositional response to dominating influences and emancipatory hope. Today there is a large critical literature in teacher education and organisation studies, and its influence continues to grow. Other research traditions have emerged from critical theory, or have been strengthened by it; for example, critical feminist research and liberation theology, as well as action research.

Critique

It is well to remember that critical theory operates from within the broad context of social science. Although its methods are appropriate to educational settings, it does not claim to be educative, that is (in Dewey's 1916 view), develop relationships which lead to further growth. The aim of critical theory is to critique, not to manage change. However, while critical theorists appear to address action and education, often they remain at the level of rhetoric, in that their theorising is limited to propositional statements rather than embodied in their own practices as they engage with issues of social change.

This is the main limitation of critical theory as a theory of social renewal. It stays at the linguistic level of description and propositional explanations. While critical theorists say what ought to be done to right wrongs, they do not show how it can be done or what needs to be done to realise the potentialities of their theories to turn them into living realities. They still cling to the reality of the model. Further, they believe that it is sufficient to critique other people but they seldom critique themselves, another example of living contradictions, and a weakness which could lead to challenges of self-righteous judgementalism.

Critical theory has amazing power for social renewal, provided critical theorists take the further step of showing how the theory works. This would mean transforming the abstract theory into concrete action plans and then acting in the direction the theory leads and producing accounts of practice to show how the critique enabled them to implement change towards improvement. Nothing could be simpler, or perhaps more difficult, because this means stepping from behind the abstract curtain into reality, and living out one's own theory in practice – not easy but entirely possible, provided one's commitments give one the courage to do so.

WHERE IS ACTION RESEARCH WITHIN THESE TYPOLOGIES?

In this section I want to say how I feel action research has the potential to generate theories of social change with regard to its knowledge base, its capacity to go beyond established human interests and its form of research as a living practice.

The knowledge base of action research

When people do action research as a living practice rather than only speak about it as a theoretical model they do not see different kinds of knowledge as separate but as integrated in their own lives. Rational know that and practical know how are integrated with and within their own personal knowing. So, for example, a counsellor might know the conceptual theory of counselling (know that) and be skilled in counselling techniques (know how), but would always go on an understanding of the person. Similarly, doctors and teachers see the whole person, and work with people on an individual basis. Knowing becomes a holistic practice; the boundaries between theory and practice dissolve and fade away, because theory is lived in practice and practice becomes a form of living theory.

Towards a new human interest

Habermas's typology of technical, practical and emancipatory interests is an E-theory which presents interests as objects of enquiry. This is not how my reality works. If I need something, or if some aspect of my life is unsatisfactory, I do not just sit and wait for something to happen. I take action. Nor do I expect anyone else to speak on my behalf or accept responsibility for my welfare.

I encourage this same attitude in my course participants. I support them carefully, but in the final analysis they have to do their own learning. I cannot do it for them. Their learning is borne out in comments such as: 'I have learnt to think for myself'; 'I have changed my thinking. I have learnt to see things as provisional. This has been difficult as I am one who tends to be comfortable with security' (taken from evaluation comments from course participants in Ireland, 2000).

I believe that the people I support have developed their own I-theories of knowledge, and I have tried to create the spaces they need to do that by not imposing my own ideas or demands on them but encouraging them to think, challenge and have confidence in their capacity to be competent judges of their own practice. Some are producing accounts to show how they are encouraging their students to do the same. Margaret Cahill (2000: 6), for example, tells of how her workplace cultures required her to teach in a manner alien to her own values: 'Imposition of content, didactic teaching strategies denied realisation of my values of justice and respect for the individual learner'. She struggled to overcome the situation, in spite of hostility to her ideas. This involved making herself vulnerable by inviting student comment on her practice, often to her cost. 'If we say anything wrong we'll get extra homework!' one brave student told her (p. 50). She persevered, however, and reached the stage where she offered to help a student, only to be informed, 'Oh, Teacher, that's OK. We looked that up ourselves' (p. 58). Reflecting on her own progress, Margaret concludes: 'I try to teach in an open questioning manner which recognises that knowledge is constructed and individual, hoping to create divergent, rather than convergent thinkers . . . This research has allowed us to arrive at an understanding of what it means to engage in truly emancipatory learning' (pp. 73–5). Margaret was awarded a distinction for the MA dissertation from which these extracts are drawn.

My own I-theory of management is that the work of an educative manager is to create such spaces so that people can work out their answers for themselves, free from constraint but confident that they will be listened to respectfully and encouraged while they develop their emergent thinking.

The metaphor I use to help me understand the nature of my own practice is one of generative transformational processes (see Chapter 3; see also McNiff, 2000). All things are in a constant state of self-renewal and change; this is the nature of life itself. Whatever exists is in a constant state of disequilibrium, a metamorphosis from one form to another, and always in life-affirming directions (although we humans often get in the way to distort the life-affirming nature of growth). I find Habermas's typology of human interests most helpful for understanding my own situation, but my practice is not fragmented. It is holistic, always responding to people, always in relation. I therefore need to develop metaphors and I-theories to communicate this reality. My preferred metaphors are those in which technical, practical and emancipatory interests are enfolded, and unfold as evolutionary processes within a holistic view of people in relation, a spiritual connectedness which enables us to recognise one another's humanity and work towards realising our own potentialities for humanity.

I think it is time to develop a new inclusive human interest of relationship which embeds and transforms itself out of the others, and show the power of this view in the way we can live our lives as creative, life-affirming processes.

Research as a form of relational practice

I am not claiming that action research is the only way to move in this direction. Much can be learnt from cultural and political workers, artists, religious leaders, and others. I am claiming, however, that action research, as a practical way of generating one's own theory of living, is a potentially powerful methodology for theories of relationship.

Although action research, like other learning processes, works at the level of the individual, it is always, like other learning processes, located in and influenced by a wider environment, including human interactions. Action research has to be participatory because the practice we are investigating is always in relation with other people. When we say we intend to improve something, there is an assumption that we are improving for a purpose, towards personal and social benefit. When we evaluate our practice this refers to the influence of our practice in other people's lives. When we generate new knowledge it is of how we are in relation to others, and the theories we produce show the process of how we have developed our practices in relationship.

To check that the practice is as we hope it to be, and make claims that we have improved, we have to produce evidence to show how we feel a situation has changed because of our influence. The process of research becomes the practice, and because we are involved in a research process of thinking, evaluating and acting, the practice is a form of research. The boundaries are dissolved; knowledge, interests and practice are integrated within a life.

HOW CAN THESE IDEAS BE DEVELOPED?

The ideas can be developed as theories of social evolution when we regard action research as something we do, not only as an abstract theory. This means developing living forms of theory which communicate how relational practices can be developed.

Propositional theory remains the dominant form for human enquiry. Many people believe it is sufficient to talk about a theory rather than live it in their own life and produce evidence to show whether it works. This keeps theory at the level of ideological fantasy (Žižek, 1990) rather than living reality. A new approach is needed.

Schön (1995), drawing on the work of Boyer (1990), calls for a new scholarship which will move beyond traditional views that see theory as a body of knowledge which can be applied to practice. Traditional research practices do not lead to personal or social change. For example (my example, not Schön's), one can read about the philosophy of education but this will not help in understanding how to motivate disaffected students or overcome one's own inertia. Schön believes that practitioners need to study their own practice and generate their own personal theories out of that practice (see also Whitehead, 1985). In doing this practitioners are drawing on their own tacit situational knowledge to help them understand how to act responsibly. The theories they generate are located in the practice, drawn from the practice, and feed back into the practice as the practitioners use new insights to act in new ways. Theory and practice are not separate entities; they are different perspectives of the same experience, rather like (to use Mary Midgley's analogy) the inside and the outside of a teapot.

In Whitehead's (1993) system of ideas the person embodies both the theory and the practice in the process of knowledge creation. The theory is not external to the person; it is within the person, as they live their life. Personal lives are always lived with other lives. Knowledge is created within the human mind-brain as it is in relation with others, so personal theories are constituted of personal knowledge as well as relational knowledge. These are living theories – of organisation, education, management, nursing, and so on; and because they are educational, in the view adopted throughout this book, they are educational theories which have the potential for personal and social renewal.

In my own work (see Chapter 3) I have developed the idea, adapted from the work of Chomsky, of generative transformational systems. The idea of knowledge creation refers to people in relationship whose collective influence enables any one knower to transform their learning into increasingly improved versions of itself. Individual learning can lead to collective learning, as people share their knowledge, and is also potentially self-transforming. The iterative exponential patterns are potentially infinite.

SO HOW DO WE COME TO KNOW?

These ideas about the generative transformational nature of living educational theories present a view of knowledge production, of personal and collective learning, as potentially endless and with potentially limitless influence for social evolution.

However, while the ideas might communicate the transformational nature of theory and learning, they do not yet address the tricky question of 'What do we need to know in order to move our enquiries forward?' This question involves issues of power and politics, and the need to break the cycle of cultural reproduction (as it exists in traditional education practices), and engage in a process of cultural interruption for cultural transformation (Grace, 1995: 13–14). To do this, we need to develop generative transformational epistemologies of practice which have compassion for the other as the heart of the matter, and regard those epistemologies of practice as the basis of our educational and social practices. This theme is taken further in Chapter 4.

Before that, Chapter 3 offers an overview of some of the most influential models of action research, and aims to show how these models reflect the different forms of theory used to describe and explain action research processes.

3   Who has influenced our thinking?

Key theorists in action research

'There are all sorts of cognitive devices – metaphor and analogy are good examples – which we use to structure and produce our knowledge of the world' (Jenkins, 1992: 56). Educational research, along with other forms of scientific enquiry, does this. Many researchers (myself included) go on to produce linguistic or visual models to communicate their ideas.

In this chapter I will look at some of the most influential models in the action research literature and examine the assumptions which underlie them. In this way we can decide whether to adopt the models or create others which will better show the values and assumptions that inform our own practices.

This presentation of key models helps to outline some of the developments in action research since the 1940s. It is not my intention to produce a comprehensive history of action research; there is not space, and good accounts already exist (Carr and Kemmis, 1986; McKernan, 1991; Noffke, 1997a). It is my intention, however, to explain how models (representations of reality) reflect forms of theory (how one thinks about reality). Dominant models, and the thinking used to produce them, are conceptual, abstract and reified (unchanging), and there are inherent limitations in this view. I will present newer models which emphasise the unpredictable nature of practitioners' work as they try to make sense of what they are doing, and show how these are generated from within a form of theory which also is fluid and dialectical. I will explain why I believe these metaphors are more appropriate for communicating the nature of educational knowledge and the processes of knowledge generation.

As noted earlier, there is today in the action research community a considerable divide between those who work at the level of abstraction and use the metaphors of a static reality and those who aim to develop new metaphors which show life and living as fluid processes. In the first view knowledge is a 'given', something to be acquired. In the second view knowledge is something which people generate for themselves as they work out their dilemmas and issues.

Consequently there is considerable debate about the methodological and epistemological bases of action research. People in the first category regard action research as a methodology which can be applied to practice; in some extreme cases action research is viewed as a method. The focus of action research is to observe behaviour and offer descriptions of what people are doing. For those in the second category, action research is a methodology that is developed from within practice, a process of trying to understand how values may be lived in practice. There is also debate between the different members of the broad action research family about the purposes of action research. Some say that the purpose of action research is to observe and describe individuals' actions in order to understand how they behave (E-theories); others say that the purpose of action research is to find ways of influencing social change through the production of descriptions and explanations by individuals themselves to account for their educational practices (I-theories). The work of key theorists in action research is now presented. Many important names in the literature are left out, a matter of space, not a denial of their influence.

EARLY INFLUENCES: THE WORK OF JOHN COLLIER AND KURT LEWIN

Susan Noffke (1997a) tells how the work of John Collier, Commissioner of Indian Affairs from 1933 to 1945, might be seen as the first identifiable starting point for action research. Collier was committed to developing 'community', as it related to education and social contexts for Native Americans, and this was to be accomplished through 'the experience of responsible democracy' (Collier, 1945: 275, cited in Noffke, 1997a: 4). Kurt Lewin, a Jewish refugee from Nazi Germany, shared the same interests as Collier, but from the perspective of industrial contexts and how participation in decision-making could lead to enhanced productivity. Collier and Lewin were aware of the potential of democratic practice for both self-determination and social engineering, the potential of 're-education' as a way of ensuring compliance and loyalty to the dominant culture.

Some historical accounts (for example, McKernan, 1991) locate the development of action research alongside other contemporary developments in education and the social sciences: the widening acceptance of new approaches in ethnography; the Science in Education movement of the nineteenth and early twentieth centuries; the Progressive Education movement, particularly the thinking of John Dewey and its practical implementation by people such as Hilda Taba and Stephen Corey; and the Group Dynamics movement in social psychology and human relations

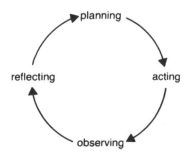

Figure 3.1 Action–reflection cycle

training. These trends had significance for the reconstruction of post-war society, in which practitioner research came to be seen as an important factor.

Lewin developed a theory of action research as a spiral of steps involving planning, fact-finding (or reconnaissance) and execution (Lewin, 1946), and which later came generally to be understood as an action–reflection cycle of planning, acting, observing and reflecting (see Figure 3.1).

This model might be understood in the following terms (my example, not Lewin's).

My context

I am a communications manager in a firm. My concern is to make communications more effective. What do I do?

Planning

I need to make communications more effective. Perhaps I could draw up and issue weekly information sheets to the staff.

Acting

I draw up and issue the information sheets.

Observing

I talk with staff who say they are now more aware of issues.

Reflecting

Do I know what they really think? How can I get feedback?

This cycle would then go on to the next cycle of replanning, acting, observing and reflecting, and perhaps produce a new cycle (Figure 3.2):

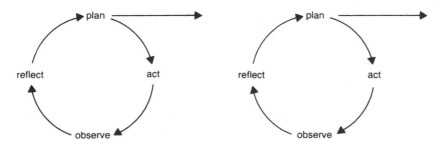

Figure 3.2 Sequences of action–reflection cycles

The cycle could continue:

Planning

Perhaps I should develop a better communication system by first finding out what people need. How to do this? A suggestions box?

Acting

I install a suggestions box.

Observing

The suggestions received are that I should (1) appoint a liaison officer; (2) hold weekly (and more democratic) staff meetings.

Reflecting

Perhaps this is a good idea. I must be careful not to lose control, though. How shall I set about becoming more democratic? Do I want to do this?

Planning

I shall invite Mrs J to be an informal liaison person. I shall publish an agenda for a staff meeting and invite staff to submit ideas.

Acting

I speak with Mrs J. I post an agenda on the staff room noticeboard.

Observing

Mrs J is hesitant because she is not clear about the brief (nor am I), but accepts provisionally. Three sensible suggestions for inclusion on the agenda arrive: issues about who has priority in bids for holiday timings; the state of the ladies' room; the need for flexitime. A further suggestion is about staff appearing in fancy dress on Christmas Eve.

Reflecting

How can I ensure that Mrs J will not feel threatened? Should I include the three sensible suggestions on the agenda, and put the fancy-dress idea under AOB? Is it such a trivial suggestion? It is to me; perhaps not for others.

So the cycle continues, showing a change in thinking as well as a change in action.

The change in thinking can also be called learning; openness to learning is a necessary condition for action research.

Lewin's work was not located primarily in education settings, and his ideas were later developed in industry and social relations (see Eden and Huxham, 1999). However, the relevance of his work to education was clear, and his ideas were soon applied in education in the USA. In 1953 Stephen Corey's book *Action Research to Improve School Practices* became highly influential. After the initial enthusiasm that this book generated, however, the idea of action research began to lose momentum, and came to be replaced by a post-Sputnik Research, Development and Diffusion model, a model much favoured in the 1960s in the USA and Britain which emphasised the separation of research and practice. It was centrally funded, and undertaken on a large scale rather than the individualised, small-scale approaches of action research. The decline of action research is well captured in the title of Nevitt Sanford's (1970) paper 'Whatever happened to action research?'

In the late 1960s a new impetus for action research developed in teacher education. An influential paper by J. J. Schwab, 'The practical: A language for the curriculum' (1969), captured the impact on education of an increasingly inward-turning mood in the USA, arising out of circumstances such as the social unease generated by civil rights movements and protests against the Korean and Vietnam wars, McCarthyism, and an increasing focus on technological control. Attention turned again to the potential of localised practitioner research as a form of educational and social change.

By now work elsewhere was becoming influential.

THE WORK OF LAWRENCE STENHOUSE

In Britain similar trends were evident in the work of Lawrence Stenhouse and the Humanities Curriculum Project. Stenhouse took as central the idea of teacher as researcher. He saw teaching and research as closely related, and called for teachers to reflect critically and systematically about their practice as a form of curriculum theorising. Teachers should be the best judges of their own practice. By accepting the responsibility for their own work, teachers could examine how they were influencing educational processes.

> all well-founded curriculum research and development, whether the work of an individual teacher, of a school, of a group working in a teacher's centre or a group working within the co-ordinating framework of a national project, is based on the study of classrooms. It thus rests on the work of teachers.
>
> (Stenhouse, 1975: 143)

Teachers therefore should aim to become extended professionals (a theme developed in the work of Hoyle, 1974; Hoyle and John, 1995), and this involved

> The commitment to systematic questioning of one's own teaching as a basis for development; the commitment to and the skills to study one's own teaching; the concern to question and to test theory in practice by the use of those skills.
>
> (Stenhouse, 1975: 144)

Stenhouse saw the work of higher-education personnel as supporting the work of teachers. Teachers were not yet encouraged to explain their own epistemological and social commitments for trying to improve their practice. Stenhouse's view was that 'fruitful development in the field of curriculum and teaching depends upon evolving styles of co-operative research by teachers and using full-time researchers to support the teachers' work' (Stenhouse, 1975: 162).

The form of theory was conceptual, the approach interpretive. The external researchers were still more powerful than the teachers they worked with. It was possible to generate E-theories about educational practices from observing how teachers behaved within their own classrooms, and to evaluate their behaviour in terms of their effectiveness in producing desired outcomes. No one yet spoke of the need for anyone to produce personal accounts of practice to check to what extent they were evaluating and theorising their own practice or living in the direction of their own educational values; this applied as much to the external researchers as to the teachers whom they were supporting.

THE SEMINAL WORK OF STEPHEN KEMMIS AND JOHN ELLIOTT

Stenhouse's ideas were further extended in the work of John Elliott and Clem Adelman in the Ford Teaching Project, 1973–1976, which was perhaps 'the greatest impetus to the resurgence of contemporary interest in educational action research' (Kemmis, 1993: 180).

> This project, initially based at the Centre for Applied Research in Education, University of East Anglia, involved teachers in collaborative action research into their own practices, in particular in the area of inquiry/discovery approaches to learning and teaching (Elliott, 1976–77). Its notion of the 'self-monitoring teacher' was based on Lawrence Stenhouse's (1975) views of the teacher as a researcher and an 'extended professional'.
>
> (Kemmis, 1993: 180–1)

Elliott has developed these ideas considerably (for example, Elliott, 1991, 1998), particularly as they relate to ideas about an objectives view and a process view of curriculum, and the social processes involved.

Other researchers gathered around Stenhouse, including Stephen Kemmis, David Hamilton, Barry MacDonald, Jean Rudduck, Hugh Sockett, Robert Stake and Rob Walker. These people did much to establish action research as an educational tradition (see, for example, Ebbutt and Elliott, 1985; MacDonald and Walker, 1976;

Rudduck and Hopkins, 1985). Some of them have further developed the field by producing influential models of action research to explain its processes.

The work of Stephen Kemmis and John Elliott has been seminal in this regard. Here I shall give a brief outline of their work, and also mention others who have adapted or refined their ideas.

Stephen Kemmis

Kemmis bases his ideas on the original conceptualisation of action research by Lewin. His work is particularly significant in understanding the socially and politically constructed nature of educational practices. Together with Wilf Carr, he has encouraged the use of the term 'educational action research' (see Carr and Kemmis, 1986), a term that has made its way onto the cover of the journal of the Collaborative Action Research Network.

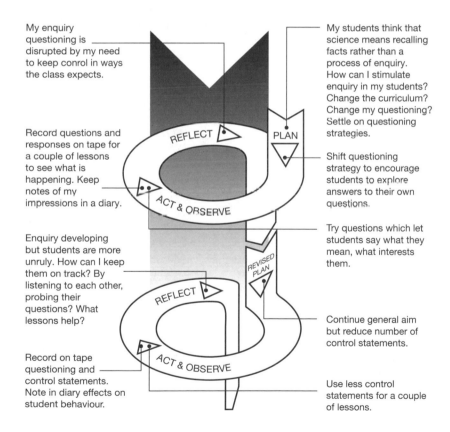

Figure 3.3 The individual aspect in action research

Source: Kemmis and McTaggart (1988)

Kemmis's model of the action research process (see Kemmis and McTaggart, 1982, and several revised editions since) shows a self-reflective spiral of planning, acting, observing, reflecting and re-planning as the basis for understanding how to take action to improve an educational situation (see Figure 3.3).

The diagram shows the principles in action, the movement from one critical phase to another, and the way in which progress may be made through systematic steps.

Here are some further examples (my examples, not Kemmis's) of mapping the steps of an action enquiry on to Kemmis's diagram. They are taken from different contexts.

Example 1: Teaching context

Planning

I am not comfortable with the textbook we are using. A lot of the material is irrelevant to the students' needs, but it is the only book available. What can I do? I can't change the book. Shall I change my way of using it? Perhaps I'll try paired work with my students.

Acting

I show the students how to ask and answer questions with each other to make the material relevant to themselves. We try this out in class.

Observing

I sit with various pairs and listen. I tape record their conversations (I got their permission to do so previously). I keep my own field notes.

Reflecting

They seem to be enjoying this, but now they wander from the material in the text. I need to get this material across.

Planning

I could get the students to develop an interview technique. A could ask B questions based on the material. I wonder would that make the material more relevant? I need to involve them more actively.

Acting

They record their conversations. There are not enough tape-recorders to go round, so they work in fours, taking it in turns to listen and talk. At the end of the two sets of interviews they listen and comment on individual recordings.

Observing

They really enjoy this. And they seem to be sticking to the text in creating their questions and answers.

Reflecting

I need to think whether I am right in teaching the content through the process. I think I am but I need to check. I'll ask my head of department who has agreed to act as my critical friend through the research project. Should I aim to do this with other classes? I am worried about the practical difficulties – too much noise? Not enough tape-recorders. Perhaps these questions are the beginning of another aspect of my original enquiry.

Example 2: Management context

Planning

As a middle manager I am responsible for improving working relationships in my firm. What can I do? Where do I begin? At the moment, what with the recent closure of a branch in the north, there is a lot of tension and mistrust of management among employees. Perhaps I should start by trying to bring people together more to talk in formal and informal contexts.

Acting

I will arrange for a series of open forum meetings with local managers in which employees can ask questions and expect clear information about future developments. I will encourage the managers to speak honestly and without anxiety.

Observing

The first meeting goes quite well. There are some tensions; one manager is defensive and some employees are aggressive, but generally there seems to be a fair exchange of views.

Reflecting

Fine so far, but exchange of points of view is not enough to create mutual trust. How do we develop the initiative?

Planning

For the second meeting I negotiate with managers and employees to form a discussion panel. All participants present their points of view. Other managers become members of the audience with a brief to listen and not interrupt.

Acting

I arrange the seating so that the panel is sitting around a table, and the rest of the audience listens. I negotiate for an employee to chair the proceedings.

Observing

The discussion is lively, with everyone showing consideration for other people's opinions. Tricky issues surface, however, and some members of the audience, employees and managers, find it difficult to respond without aggression.

Reflecting

Perhaps I need to find ways of involving people more in the planning of the meetings. Perhaps I could negotiate spokespersons rather than invite everyone to speak in an arbitrary manner.

It is frequently the case in action research that other ideas and problem areas arise that are not the main focus of the research but are relevant and need to be dealt with to facilitate progress of the main focus. Kemmis's model is unable to deal with this spontaneity and untidiness. The model is presented as if life goes along one path only, in a linear sequence. This is not the way things usually happen. The model does not recognise the existence of related issues, nor present options for dealing with them: what did he do about his 'need to keep control in ways that the class expects'?

My critique is to do with methodological and epistemological issues. I know that Stephen Kemmis's contributions to action research are considerable, and he has influenced policy-makers worldwide in supporting educators and improving educational opportunities.

John Elliott

John Elliott is an active supporter of educators across a variety of professions. He is well known, for example, for his support of police work, and is currently active in a wide range of international contexts in developing policy to encourage participation in education in various contexts. Until recently he was the co-ordinator of the Collaborative Action Research Network. His work in curriculum theorising is highly influential (see, for example, Elliott, 1998), and he continues the tradition, established by Stenhouse, of moving from an objectives focus to a process focus in curriculum theorising.

Like Kemmis, Elliott agrees with the basic action–reflection spiral of cycles, but presents his own critique:

> Although I think Lewin's model is an excellent basis for starting to think about what action research involves, it can . . . allow those who use it to assume that 'the general idea' can be fixed in advance, that 'reconnaissance' is merely

fact-finding, and that 'implementation' is a fairly straightforward process. But I would argue that:

- The general idea should be allowed to shift.
- Reconnaissance should involve analysis as well as fact-finding and should constantly recur in the spiral of activities, rather than occur only at the beginning.
- Implementation of an action step is not always easy, and one should not proceed to evaluate the effects of an action until one has monitored the extent to which it has been implemented.

(Elliott, 1991: 70)

He goes on to present a new model (see Figure 3.4).

The work of Kemmis and Elliott has influenced others. Notable researchers include the following:

David Ebbutt

David Ebbutt agrees generally with the ideas of Kemmis and Elliott, but disagrees (1985) about some of Elliott's interpretations of Kemmis's work. He claims that the spiral is not necessarily the most useful way in which to describe the action–reflection process.

He also raises issues (as I am doing) about the logic of action research. He points out the difference between theorising about systems and putting those systems into operation in real life:

I had made the assumptions that Elliott's logic and Kemmis's maxims were being used synonymously to describe the same thing. But as I now understand it, maxims are little more than rule of thumb, or rules of the art. Maxim . . . tells us something about successfully operationalizing action research but it does not determine the practice of action research. Maxim . . . has been derived empirically by successful practitioners of action research, whereas the logic of action research determines the practice upon which they came to engage.

(Ebbutt, 1985: 172)

James McKernan

James McKernan links action research with curriculum research and development. His *Curriculum Action Research: A Handbook of Methods and Resources for the Reflective Practitioner* (1991) is written from an externalist and quite instrumental perspective. 'Research is a method,' he states unequivocally (p. 34). Some would suggest that research is far more than a method. Building on Kemmis's work, he produces a diagram of sequential spirals and suggests a 'time process' model. It is important, he says, not to let a 'problem' become fixed in time, but to build in the necessary flexibility to allow the focus to shift and innovative episodes to occur.

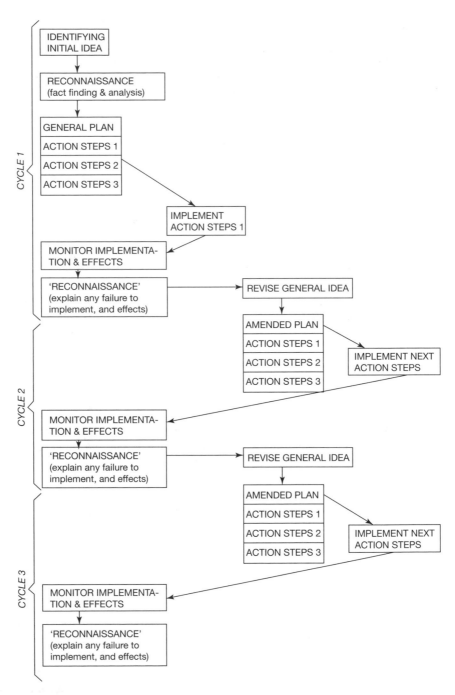

Figure 3.4 Revised version of Lewin's model of action research
Source: Elliott (1991)

Ortrun Zuber-Skerritt

Writing from a critical theoretic perspective, as well as from an externalist perspective, Ortrun Zuber-Skerritt links action research with professional learning in higher education (1992a and b) and organisational change and management development (1996). She presents her CRASP model:

Action research is:

Critical (and self-critical) collaborative enquiry by
Reflective practitioners being
Accountable and making the results of their enquiry public,
Self-evaluating their practice and engaged in
Participative problem-solving and continuing professional development.
(Zuber-Skerritt, 1992b: 15; emphases in original)

The works are liberally illustrated with sophisticated and elaborate diagrams to show the process on paper. One can only wonder whether the process can be realised in real life and what might be its educational impact when it is.

Critical reflection

Several criticisms could be advanced in response to the models presented so far. I shall confine my critique to the assumptions which underpin the models in terms of their lack of contact with practice, particularly as this shows in (a) their prescriptiveness, (b) their ignoring of the values base of practice and (c) their sociological rather than educational perspective.

The prescriptiveness of models

Bourdieu (1990) has several concerns about how three-dimensional practice is presented in two-dimensional visual form. One concern is that model-makers do not emphasise that their model is only their idea, not some kind of universal 'given'. While diagrams aim to communicate the vision of the designer that this is how reality works, he says, there is often slippage between the diagram and reality. This particularly applies to diagrams that communicate reality as sequential and predictable (as per the models presented so far in this chapter). Such diagrams are produced as synopses of events. Bourdieu calls this a 'synoptic illusion' because the model of reality does not necessarily communicate people's experience of reality. A calendar, for example, does not communicate the reality of a life lived in real time. Bourdieu does, however, hold out the possibility of constructing 'a simple generative model which makes it possible to give an account of the logic of practice' (p. 100). Such a model 'generates an infinity of practices adapted to situations that are always different' (p. 101). Whitehead's model (Chapter 5) and my own (see p. 57) aim to do this. A model which communicates dialectical processes is more appropriate to the fluidity and unpredictability of practical living and the improvisatory knowledge base which underpins it.

An inherent assumption of propositional models is that practice can be portrayed as linear and sequential, neat and orderly. This frequently is not so. Con Ó Muimhneacháin shows this in his story (Chapter 10 of this book) when he describes how he encountered opposition to his ideas, and how he then became aware that action research involves understanding how to make sense of practice when things go wrong as much as when they go as planned. Agnes Higgins (2000) also makes the point that prescriptive model-makers tend to assume that practice will follow the model: however, 'Action does not proceed in a fixed linear fashion' (p. 134) and the assumption that she would produce a report as if it did potentially distorted the reality of her practice.

> Hence telling the story in a concise and coherent manner without losing sight of the confusion and human dimension that was such a part of the process was a major challenge. Given the open systemic nature of organisations and the diversity of people involved, a variety of issues arose during each cycle that influenced progress and demanded that we return to previous stages.
>
> (Higgins, 2000: 134)

As in many things we might like to think that we can predict and control the future, but reality says differently. I return to my certainty of uncertainty. While I believe that models and other metaphors can offer useful indicators of how things might go, model-makers need to emphasise to an unsuspecting public that these are fantasies, a first step, a useful technique, in understanding how one might proceed. Further, if model-makers aim to claim theoretical validity for their models they need to go beyond the level of speculation and also present stories of their own real-world practice to show how the models informed their own progress (or lack of it). They need to aim for explanatory adequacy, to produce both descriptions and explanations for their own practice and show how they live out their metaphors. Practitioners should be advised that they do not have to follow the models, for the models are not necessarily representative of the realities practitioners will experience. Practitioners need to see these models for what they are: guidelines for how we hope things will eventually fall out. To propose that action research models can be imposed on practice is to turn action research into a technology, an oppressive instrument which can potentially distort other people's creative practice.

Ignoring the values base of practice

The world is full of official rhetoric. This rhetoric translates easily into prescriptive charts and documents. An example of this is the Teacher Training Agency's (1998) outline of the skills necessary for demonstrating professional expertise – if we show that we can perform according to a prescriptive checklist of skills we have passed the test. Practice is then taken to be a performance, the execution of technical tasks.

This is an approach much loved by sociologists who observe the world and interpret other people's behaviour. Sociological analysis (often in terms of know that) is, however, separated from educational understanding (often in terms of practical wisdom) by a gulf, and the nature of the gulf is an empty space occupied by the sociologist as a faceless person. Sociologists frequently do not recognise themselves, or make themselves visible, as part of the same reality as those whose lives they are describing; they prefer to keep their distance as external researchers.

I am not critiquing sociology as a form of enquiry. I am saying that, while sociological analysis from the perspective of an external researcher might provide important insights into the formation of social practices, it is not the most appropriate way to explain or understand practice, educational practice in particular. For educational enquiry to move from E-approaches to I-approaches, people have to produce their own accounts of practice to show how they are living in the direction of their values, intentions and purposes. Education is predicated on values. How we act depends on what we believe we are acting for. Purposes and practices are always linked. Are we living to fulfil other people's expectations or our own? Is someone else writing the script, or are we? Who creates our identities, and for what purposes? The propositional knowledge base of sociological analysis is different from the dialectical knowledge base of personal practice. In other words, the epistemological basis of social scientific theories is different from the epistemological basis of living theories.

Keeping education in educational research

In his essay 'Why educational research has been so uneducational: The case for a new model of social science based on collaborative inquiry' William Torbert (1981) investigates the gap between educational theory and educational practice. 'Why hasn't past educational research taught us better educational practice?' he asks, and suggests that 'the reasons why neither current practice nor current research helps us to identify and move towards good educational practice is that both are based on a model of reality that emphasises unilateral control for gaining information from, or having effects on, others' (p. 142).

Action research is a form of researching one's learning. Because it is always done with others, it is important to ensure that relationships are of a kind that will lead to education. The purpose of education, says Dewey (1916), is to lead to further education; that is, education is a process of growth whose purpose is to sustain growth. Learning how to do this is part of a process which can be called educational.

When people undertake action research they aim to improve their work, and because their work is always work with others, the implication is that they are improving their understanding of how better to live with others so that all participants in the process can grow. Action research in most definitions appears as a process of improving one's own understanding of how to improve social situations. This implies improving personal and collective relationships – the process of education.

It does not make sense, therefore, to adopt forms of theory which legitimate a relationship in which some persons act and others watch or direct – shades of the empiricist agenda of predict and control. Educational means education for all. The idea of educational research implies a process in which all are prepared to grow, not a process in which one who is already grown tells another how to do it.

Research which encourages practitioners to investigate their own practice on the job and share their insights can be educational, in that it attempts to help people make sense of their own realities and account for their own learning. They can say why they felt the need to evaluate and improve practice. They can present evidence to show how they have improved their own understanding of their practice, and possibly the practice itself. This kind of approach enables practitioners to claim that working with others has been an educative process, and has enabled them to generate and test with others their own emergent theories of education and practice towards personal and social renewal.

DIALECTICAL APPROACHES: JACK WHITEHEAD AND HIS IDEA OF LIVING EDUCATIONAL THEORIES

While Lawrence Stenhouse was working on the Humanities Curriculum Project, and John Elliott and Clem Adelman were developing the Ford Teaching Project, Jack Whitehead at the University of Bath was working with teachers as part of the Schools Council Mixed Ability Exercise in Science. He was studying his own practice of supporting teachers in their science enquiries.

Throughout his project, Whitehead has aimed to develop a form of theory different from received propositional forms. Since the 1970s his aim has been to have the form of theory legitimated by the Academy, and that has now been accomplished, with significant numbers of practitioners having received their masters and doctoral degrees around the world through studying their own practices and showing how they can make claims to have improved the quality of that practice for others' benefit. The focus of his work has now shifted from legitimation for the form of theory to finding ways of influencing thinking at world level (www.actionresearch.net).

Jack's approach goes beyond dominant E-approaches. He adopts rather an I-approach, which encourages practitioners themselves to produce their own descriptions and explanations for their own learning. They do this by undertaking their action enquiries into their own practice, producing evidence to show that they have improved practice, and having that evidence validated by the critical scrutiny of others. This is a highly rigorous process (as described in some detail in Chapter 5).

A focus of his own project is the generic question 'How do I improve my practice?' (Whitehead, 1989, 1998, 2000). In attempting to respond to this question, Jack is developing an epistemology of practice that takes the idea of the 'I' as a living contradiction in the sense that he believes in certain values yet finds himself sometimes living in ways which deny those values (see, for example, D'Arcy, 1998;

see also Lomax *et al.*, 1999). Overcoming the contradiction so that he can be said to be living his values in practice is a key aspect of the enquiry, the substantive content of his own learning as he seeks to become a better educator.

Jack regards educational enquiry as distinctively different from present forms of social scientific enquiry. 'The inclusion of "I" as a living contradiction in educational enquiries can lead to the creation of research methodologies which are distinctively "educational" and cannot be reduced to social science methodologies' (Whitehead, 2000: 93). Social scientific enquiries lead to knowledge about the world, as they are conducted from the perspective of external researchers who are aiming to understand and describe a situation as an object of study (and develop E-theories). Educational enquiries (I-systems of knowledge) lead to knowledge of self within a world which the researcher co-creates with others who are similarly occupied (and develop I-theories of practice). The reflective practice which characterises these efforts is a form of practical theorising which can lead to the evolution of good social orders.

DEVELOPING GENERATIVE TRANSFORMATIONAL APPROACHES TO EDUCATIONAL ENQUIRY

I said in the Introduction that I had developed comfort in insecurity. Ten years ago my life was mapped out. I would have done X by Y date; I would move systematically along a given trajectory towards a predesignated closure. During those ten years most of what was planned has been disrupted; most of my stable points of reference dissolved. This has led to extreme dislocation, which in turn has developed into intense awareness of living in the moment. I now hold my dreams lightly, and they are precious but not indestructible, and I walk in gratitude that I am here at all. I no longer take things for granted.

This process of personal turbulent destabilisation in life experience has helped my capacity to theorise my own practice as a learner and a teacher, and, in the context of this book, to understand my own practice as an action researcher.

In earlier times, when I first became involved in action research, I was much attracted to the propositional ideas of Kemmis and Elliott, but I soon found that they did not reflect the reality of my professional life and its hurly-burly nature. They therefore did not give me an opportunity to explain how and why I was practising as I was. I resisted the prescriptiveness of their models, and came to develop my own.

Several major themes have developed, including the need for explanatory adequacy in educational research and the need for a form of theory with generative transformational capacity. A theory which is interesting and has potential for developing new forms of understanding cannot be static; it has to be developmental, capable of turning into new forms which are already latent within the present form. The theory itself has to demonstrate its own capacity for growth in life-enhancing directions – in one sense, therefore, this has to be a theory which is inherently educational.

I learned much from studying the work of Noam Chomsky: about a centuries-long interest in the generative transformational nature of organic systems. The metaphors which best described these ideas I found in the literature of the new science, which emphasises the creative and spontaneous aspects of living as they are communicated, for example, through the patterns of fractals. I was and remain interested in how order can evolve from chaos, and in understanding the nature of chaos itself as containing a simple implicate order (Bohm, 1983) which underlies evolutionary processes (see McNiff, 2000, where I have explored these issues in depth).

I have consistently been fascinated and in complete awe of how living systems rest on a finite number of components that are capable of producing an infinite number of novel phenomena. A grammar contains a finite number of elements which in use may generate an infinite number of original utterances; a fixed number of mathematical principles – adding, multiplying, subtracting, dividing – can produce an infinite number of computations; a fixed number of facial components – eyes, nose, mouth, ears – can produce an infinite number of human faces; an acorn has the potential to become an oak tree. We all have the potential to be more than we are. Who we become depends on who we are now, and who we decide we want to be (provided, of course, that politics does not intrude, which it tends to, and distorts those potentials). We have the potential to recreate ourselves. Research has this same capacity for self-regeneration. It is the responsibility of those positioned as having educational mandates to ensure that people are able to realise their own capacity for self-recreation, and to remove obstacles which might obstruct this self-development. I am committed to these ideas, possibly because I have had to recreate myself over the past ten years, and now see that process of recreation not as a response *in extremis*, but as a voluntary form of life which follows the natural order of things. Each day, each moment, is a new creation.

In developing my own theory of the nature of action research, I have come to see it as a spontaneous, self-recreating system of enquiry. I like the notion of a systematic process of observe, describe, plan, act, reflect, evaluate, modify, but I do not see the process as sequential or necessarily rational. It is possible to begin at one place and end up somewhere entirely unexpected. The visual metaphor I have developed is an iterative spiral of spirals, an exponential developmental process. I have come to see the process as beyond words, and while I can analyse it in terms of an action research approach, I do not think it should be so confined. In my diagram (Figure 3.5) the spirals of action reflection unfold from themselves and fold back again into themselves. They attempt to communicate the idea of a reality which enfolds all its previous manifestations yet which is constantly unfolding into new versions of itself, constantly in a state of balance within disequilibrium. I am certain of uncertainty; I am balanced within my own disequilibrium. In action research terms it is possible to address multiple issues while still maintaining a focus on one, a realisation of Plato's idea of holding together the one and the many.

To show the development in my own thinking, look at the 1988 version of the model (Figure 3.6).

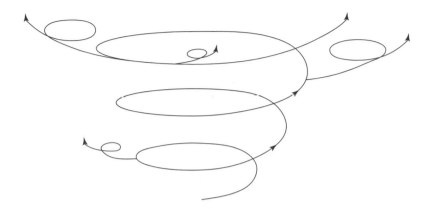

Figure 3.5 A generative transformational evolutionary process

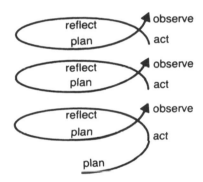

Figure 3.6 An aspect of the original 1988 diagram of a generative transformational evolutionary process

I felt then it was important to put in the action–reflection steps, something which many people have rightly criticised over the years, saying that this was too prescriptive. I now have the courage of my own comfort in insecurity to present an image of non-definitive fluidity.

Am I being prescriptive now? Or am I perhaps meeting Bourdieu's idea of a simple generative model which preserves the fluidity of practical logic? I believe this is so. I hope I am moving beyond the synoptic illusion by developing a metaphor of enquiry in action which mirrors the liberating experience of an action enquiry process.

So who has influenced our thinking?

Here is another visual synopsis to show the state of the art (see Figure 3.7), not to prescribe how things might develop (though I know how I would like them to develop, and will say so in Chapter 4).

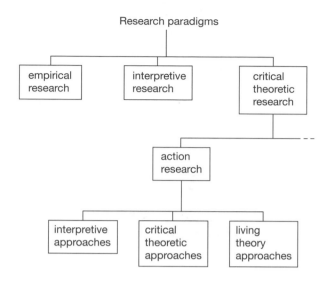

Figure 3.7 Emergent traditions in research paradigms

Within the broad arena of educational research, different paradigms exist (see Chapter 2): the empirical, the interpretive and the critical theoretic. The critical theoretic paradigm has been largely responsible for generating action research as a form of enquiry (along with other research programmes such as feminist research and liberation theology).

Over recent years three different approaches to action research have developed: an interpretive approach, a critical theoretic approach and a living theory approach. In this chapter I have suggested that the development of living theory constitutes a sharp departure from traditional forms, on a par with the second cognitive revolution of the 1950s in its move away from the descriptive E-theories of the social sciences (and educational enquiry as it is understood to be located in the social sciences), and demonstrating a commitment to the development of explanatory I-theories of education. In this view education constitutes its own discipline within the broad range of human enquiry.

Possible development of these ideas now appears in Chapter 4.

4   What do we need to know?

How can we develop our work?

Action research has significant potential for human betterment. While the term 'action research' might be superseded or embedded within newer forms of research, what it stands for is durable.

What action research stands for is the realisation of human needs towards autonomy, loving relationships and productive work; the urge towards freedom, creativity and self-recreation. The political counterpart of action research is liberal democracy; the spiritual counterpart a sense of unity between self and the cosmos. Such arenas cannot be investigated using only the traditional E-forms of the social sciences. The form of theory appropriate for such investigation is already in the mind of the person, in that each person is able to say, 'I understand what I am doing and why I am doing it.' The theory is embodied within and generated through practice (Whitehead, 2000). Studying our practice and its underpinning assumptions enables us to develop a creative understanding of ourselves and our own processes of learning and growth. When we do action research we make our thinking different. 'Having made a discovery, I shall never see the world again as before. My eyes have become different; I have made myself into a person seeing and thinking differently. I have crossed a gap, a heuristic gap which lies between problem and discovery' (Polanyi, 1958: 143).

Here I want to talk about the evolution of knowledge, and how it can lead to an evolution of practice. What do we need to know in order to realise the potentials of what action research stands for at a personal and collective level, and how do we translate that knowledge into purposeful collective action? It is important also to be aware of the existence of powerful forces which might try to suppress personal and collective renewal, and why they do so, and to show the need to develop political strength and will to circumvent these forces and develop the visions of renewal in practical ways.

This chapter, therefore, is organised in terms of the significance of what action research stands for, for the individual, for communities and for the wider field of education; and how to let that potential significance transform into influence.

Individual development

In these days of professional accountability, practitioners need to demonstrate that they are capable and competent. A heavy emphasis is placed on research-based evidence, both for institutions (in education settings this is particularly visible in the school effectiveness and improvement literatures) and for individuals (see, for example, Hargreaves, 1996). The need for practitioner excellence and account- ability goes without saying, as well as the need to produce empirical evidence to support claims that one knows what one is doing and takes responsibility for the ongoing improvement of practice. If we are not good at our jobs, or prepared to improve where necessary, we ought not to be doing the job. This presents a problem. The kind of knowledge which counts in advanced technologised societies is technical rationality, knowledge of facts and figures and how to use them. In this view, the purposes of education are systematically rewritten as knowing how to make a profit and gain competitive advantage, a leaning, in Aristotelian terms, towards *techne* (excellence in skilful making) rather than *phronesis* (excellence in wise practice). However, the two need to be seen as in balance, not competi- tion; skills are embedded within practice. Will Hutton's work is instructive here. He explains how commitment to *techne* alone does not lead to social benefit or sustainable economic well-being, but has to be embedded within a communitarian values base: 'If a well-functioning market economy requires skilled workforces, strong social institutions like schools and training centres, and a vigorous public infrastructure, these cannot be achieved if the governing class cannot understand the values implicit in such bodies' (Hutton, 1996: 25).

Today education is technologised in many of its forms. Knowledge has become a commodity and the process of knowledge production a for-profit business (Grace, 1995; Smyth and Shacklock, 1998). In the midst of the mad rush towards excellence (whatever that means) few people stop to ask, 'Excellence for what? Knowledge for whom?' Some thoughtful researchers (for example, Slee *et al.*, 1998) step out of the pressure in order to ask critical questions about knowledge production and its uses: 'What do we know? What do we need to know? Who for? Why?'

It is precisely these questions which practitioners ask as they study their own practice. They identify the values which inspire them to live as they do, and they set in motion a rigorous evaluation process to ensure the validity of their claims to knowledge, to know that they are good practitioners and are demonstrating profes- sional responsibility. Professionalism – in this view, extended professionalism (Hoyle, 1974) – is not only responsibility to others, but also responsibility to truth. There is something untruthful about current drives towards marketisation in which humanity is reduced to a technology and relationships are embittered by overt competition (although the truth of the power of the makers of such policies is beyond doubt). It is somehow an unfaithfulness to the idea of what it means to be human.

I have already noted that some theorists are turning action research into a tech- nology. This is dangerous, for action research is then seen as a set of techniques to be applied to practice rather than a way of life which constitutes practice. In this view the procedures of action research can lead to improvement of practices which can encourage social evil as well as good. There is nothing at a procedural level to stop practitioners asking, 'How can I become a more effective terrorist?' This is perfectly feasible when people follow prescriptive models which emphasise procedure, without equally emphasising the reasons and intentions which inform practice. And even when the reasons and intentions are emphasised, there is still no barrier to using an action research methodology to ask, 'How do I improve my practice as a thief?' Thieves have values the same as philanthropists, and libraries of books exist about which form of values are held in the wider courts about what counts as 'right'.

There are no easy answers. Perhaps, as indicated in Chapter 1, action research belongs to people who are already of a certain inclination, people who are already concerned about issues of social justice and participative living. Theirs is a morally committed practice, a kind of praxis. They are able to produce rigorously validated claims that they are producing knowledge which will have significance for personal and social well-being. This is not a pipe-dream. The networks of practitioners around the world who are adopting an action research approach are systematically producing coherent bodies of case-study evidence to show that their claims to educational knowledge have the potential for social change, and these stories tell of how they are influencing social systems at local, regional and national levels. How then to strengthen the influence, so that the knowledge generated through personal enquiry can be widely acknowledged as a kind of knowledge which will help towards the development of sustainable good social orders? How also to persuade others of a more technical inclination that this is a good way to be?

Community development

Two steps are important: first, the systematic production of case studies to show the development of communities of learners within organisational settings, and the kind of knowledge they are generating collectively for wider social benefit; second, efficient forms of dissemination so that these case studies cannot be overlooked and have to be acknowledged as a legitimate form of collective knowing.

It has been said (for example by Noffke, 1997b) that while action research has significant potential for personal renewal, there is doubt about its potential for organisational development. This doubt might have been understandable ten years ago; today it is not. Clear empirical evidence exists to show how individuals' enquiries into their own practice have influenced the quality of learning and action within their institutional settings (for example Dodd, 2001). The question has transformed from 'How do I improve my practice?' to 'How do we improve our practice?' People have accepted the collective responsibility of improving their own workplace practices for social benefit.

Critiques such as Noffke's are made from within one form of knowledge, the E-approaches of abstract theorising. On paper it is difficult to show the kinds of transformations in personal thinking and communication which generate social change; no synopsis can do this. Much advice exists to spell out what needs to be done (for example Zuber-Skerritt, 1996), but the limitations of conceptual forms of theory do not allow for the emergence of real-world descriptions and explanations which show what people did and how they experienced their own transformative processes. The work of Jack Whitehead and myself and the researcher communities we support tries to do this, and Jack is also currently investigating the limitations of linguistic presentations, and concentrating on using multimedia to show the living realities of transformative processes (Whitehead, forthcoming). It is impossible for E-approaches to show how change begins in individuals' minds as they examine their practice and resolve to improve it in line with their values base. How can they show the quality of relationship that is necessary to influence others? Social change was never mandated, nor did it ever begin with prescriptive models. John Hume, former leader of the SDLP in Northern Ireland, says that the peace process begins in people's minds. This is so of all social change; it happens because individuals decide to come together, wanting to change themselves and influence others also to change themselves.

I like this passage from Chomsky (1996: 77):

> The ideas expressed in the not very distant past by such outstanding figures as Russell and Dewey are rooted in the Enlightenment and classical liberalism, and retain their evolutionary character: in education, the workplace, and every other sphere of life. If implemented, they would help clear the way to the free development of human beings whose values are not accumulation and domination, but independence of mind and action, free association on terms of equality, and cooperation to achieve common goals. Such people would share Adam Smith's contempt for the 'mean' and 'sordid pursuits' of 'the masters of mankind' and their 'vile maxim': 'All for ourselves, and nothing for other people', the guiding principles we are taught to admire and revere, as traditional values are eroded under unremitting attack.

The ideas of collective commitment to social change are perfectly realisable, though not easy, but only if it is appreciated that their realisation is located within individual lives, as people aim to integrate theory and practice. In dominant epistemologies the process of theory generation is still held to be a conceptual practice, the creation of ideas about what can and cannot be done; it ignores the need for concrete theories of action, rooted in a strong values base of truth, justice and social welfare, to show how ideas can be turned into reality. The situation is changing. The case studies cited in this book, for example, show how individuals generated their own theories of knowledge, in company with others. These stories were critiqued and validated, a shared process, and many people came to influence others, who then began to undertake their own action enquiries. In some cases the patterns of individual enquiry have developed into patterns of collective enquiry, showing how people who share the common pursuits of truth and justice can develop the expertise and political wisdom to influence the socio-political cultures in which they work.

The still-dominant epistemology leads us to understand concepts such as theory, organisation and development as abstractions. They are linguistic concepts divorced from real lives. As long as they remain linguistic concepts, sustainable social change remains a chimera. Turn them into living realities, however, and the process can become real: theorising becomes a practice, organisation becomes people, development becomes the process of purposeful social action through reflection. It is not a case of people looking outside themselves for theories of living; the theories are already latent in themselves and await articulation and refinement through living.

In this talk of change what really needs changing is our thinking, particularly our ways of thinking about what kind of theory is best suited to realise our personal and social hopes. If we really want to change our situations, we need to engage with forms of knowledge and knowledge production which not only exist on paper but also have their meaning in the way we live our lives.

Educational theorising

The way to social change is through people's hearts and minds. Oonagh O'Brien (2000) speaks of the process as 'one heart at a time'. This is right, emphasising as it does the long-term and labour-intensive nature of change processes. Change begins because people see the sense of changing and want to do it.

Perhaps the most important change needs to take place in the kind of theory used for theorising educational processes. This has implications for the users of dominant theory, since the form of theory with its agenda of control and colonisation reinforces users' own positions as entitled to control and colonise, one of the reasons possibly that it is the form of theory beloved by institutions. I know several colleagues who have been promoted within higher education and other corporate scenarios who seem quite quickly to embrace bureaucratic values over educational ones. Perhaps it is something endemic to institutional life.

The Academy is still recognised within the culture as the highest body for the legitimation of knowledge. It sets what counts as the paradigmatic nature of knowledge and knowledge generation. Interesting reconceptualisations are taking place right now, however, in terms of how the university is both physically and also intellectually configured (Field and Leicester, 2000). The university is changing its shape and location, with the increasing development of off-site courses and flexible learning arrangements. The Open University is a good example. My own context is that I run accredited courses in Ireland. I live in England and visit Ireland regularly, at which time my car becomes my office. The university is solidly in the people, while my organisational location is virtual. I have to be well organised in my planning and delivery of courses, but the benefits of personal freedom and being able to meet people in their own locations are enormous. Jack Whitehead's context is that he is based in a university building, but is in touch with networks of practitioners at other university and workplace-based locations around the world. While he travels extensively to meet people on a regular basis, and works closely with local organisers, he is also constantly in touch electronically. No one is bound any more by the physical constraints of time and place, though they are often bound by their own degree of confidence in whether they are prepared to handle the freedom to think for themselves or create their own lives.

Further developments are also taking place in the whole idea of accreditation. Increasingly, private colleges and industry are achieving the right to deliver courses leading to the public recognition of their own degrees. The hegemony of the traditional university is also challenged by organisations, particularly in industry, who see that the kind of abstract knowledge valued by the Academy is becoming obsolete in terms of today's needs, together with traditional views that the only thing managers and teachers need to know is how to deliver a pre-packaged form of knowledge.

> Paradoxically, it is the technical and functional orientation to management education, with its reductionist approach, which is most criticized by practising managers in both the USA and the UK for being least relevant to their problems. It would appear that managers want management schools to offer more than technical trouble-shooting; rather, they want them to offer theories and ideas which address wider problems.
>
> (Fox, 1997: 23)

There is currently a groundswell of opinion and action to present new forms of knowledge and new contexts for knowledge production within newly articulated purposes of knowledge generation. Castells (1997) and others speak of how information has come to be reconceptualised not as a commodity for exchange, but as residing in people who generate their own knowledge which they use for their own and others' benefit. Knowledge and power are closely interlinked, as Foucault (1980) explains. How may people be helped to see the potential of their own capacity to generate their own knowledge from within their practice in order to improve their own and others' lives? How may a recognition of the need for new kinds of theory within the still-dominant technical rationality of the Academy be developed?

There are two main strategies. One is to engage with issues of theory in the domain of debate and persuasion, usually through the production of texts (as I am doing here). The more texts that appear, the stronger the influence, particularly when the texts contain concrete evidence of how people have decided for themselves to develop new ways of living. The second way is to work with practitioners at all levels of organisational systems, and encourage them to develop confidence in their own capacities to know and explain their own educational practices, and to put their accounts of the process of personal and institutional change into the public domain for critical scrutiny. This building up of a critical mass is essential, for people cannot then be ignored, even though powerful elites may try to diminish what they have to offer.

All this takes energy and commitment, not only from those initially positioned as educational leaders, but also from the whole community who have to recognise their own potentials as leaders. We lead as our personal strengths emerge at the time. We are all in this together. It is no use expecting someone else to do it – this takes us back to E-theorising. We have to do it for ourselves, recognising our own capacity for self-determination, and exercising our collective power to realise it.

Potential constraints

No one should ever lose sight of the inherent danger of challenging the establishment. The work of Bourdieu and Chomsky is particularly instructive here. Referring to the work of Bourdieu (1993), Kathleen Lynch (2000) explains how what counts as knowledge is carefully controlled in higher education contexts (while Bourdieu was writing specifically in a French context, there is good reason to believe that his insights travel well to others):

> intellectuals work in institutions which lay down working conditions based on the dominant meritocratic principles of our time – ostensibly at least, promotion is based on merit. The way in which merit is measured is in terms of conformity to the dominant norms of intellectual and academic discourse. This includes not only writing within the dominant paradigm (Kuhn, 1970) but writing about what is currently intellectually fashionable. Without at least a nodding recognition of the importance of the dominant discourses, then, one's work is not likely to be published. And it is through their publications that intellectuals in universities are generally assessed. While 'there is something desperate in the docility with which "free intellectuals" rush to hand in their essays on the required subject of the moment' (Bourdieu, 1993: 43) the fact remains that academics' jobs and incomes are often dependent on such conformity.
>
> (Lynch, 2000: 69–70)

Throughout his political writings Chomsky explains how, in totalitarian societies, it is easy enough to control people through overt systems of terror. In democratic societies, however, it is necessary to resort to the more subtle terrorism of thought control, and this is achieved through the development of elegant propaganda systems which communicate messages through the culture. The formal education system, according to Chomsky, is a system of imposed ideas; and, according to Bourdieu, is the most powerful aspect of the culture as a means for social reproduction: teaching produces students as consumers who expect to teach and be taught in a certain way. How people come to know through conventional teaching methodologies is lasting; they effectively learn not to question. Education is used as a means of controlling the thinking of consumers.

History is full of stories of people who are systematically silenced and made invisible because they disagreed with dominant voices. Anyone undertaking action research should be aware of the risks. Anderson and Herr (1999) insightfully tell how many higher education institutions are aware of the rising tide of action research, and so have to accept it in principle so as not to appear behind the times, but they allow it only in a domesticated form which does not upset dominant elites. I know of many universities who allow an ethnographic approach to action research as part of course syllabuses, probably because (see Chapter 3) this approach still maintains control of practitioners' thinking and action and so reinforces the position of the Academy as the locus of real knowledge. I also know of universities who do not allow action research at all, though I expect that shortly these will simply have to acknowledge some form of action research to maintain a modern image and to attract customers who want to do action research. Some people travel considerable distances to attend my courses because they cannot find other universities in their own locations who could offer living theory approaches to action research. It is not only anomalous but in my opinion outrageous that universities still position themselves as those-who-know and refuse to meet the needs of people who want to have their own knowing valued.

So what do we need to know? How can we develop our work?

We need to know that we are right in developing forms of personal enquiry. We need to have confidence in our own sense that learning is always undertaken by an individual, and that it is a process of investigating what is already in the mind and bringing that to consciousness for critical examination through a process of critical discernment, and then developing and refining the knowledge in company with others. The development and refining processes are undertaken within practice; by examining practice and checking that it is a living-out of the values that exist as part of the I-belief system of the knower, a knower is able to modify their practice so that it does become a living-out of values. We need to know that we are right in claiming that we understand our practice, claims made out of a sense of responsibility to the truth and justice of our relationships with one another. We need to know that these claims are rooted in our personal learning from experience, and should be tested against the best critique of others similarly engaged to establish their legitimacy.

This is Polanyi's approach to validity, when he says (1958) that it is the act of commitment in its full structure that saves personal knowledge from being merely subjective. He says that an intellectual commitment is a responsible decision, an act of hope, which is expressed in the universal intent of personal knowledge. Any conclusion, whether given as a surmise or claimed as a certainty, represents a commitment of the person who arrives at it. No one can utter more than a responsible commitment of their own, and this completely fulfils their responsibility for finding the truth and telling it. Whether or not it is the truth can be hazarded only by another, equally responsible commitment.

We need also to know that we are always in company with others. There is no getting away from this, situated as we all are as social beings. The knowledge we produce is located within our individual practice and needs to be shared with others, as it impacts on them. While knowledge production is initially always and inevitably a phenomenon of an individual mind, the development of that knowledge and its use then becomes a social process. How the knowledge is refined and shaped according to the purposes that the individual and their companions identify is a matter of negotiation, as suits their identified purposes. They then develop their community knowledge. This can never be a coercive practice, since negotiating what counts as knowledge has to be a shared practice as it communicates democratically agreed values (while some values might be contested, other values to do with shared communication and respect for others' opinions have to inform communicative action). This implies that relations need to be of the kind to encourage communication and agreement to disagree within a wider commitment to purposeful and beneficial social change (see also MacIntyre, 1990). The way that knowledge is refined and developed, according to its agreed purposes, is a relational practice. The knowledge, as it originally existed within the individual, now comes to reside within relationships, as they are communicated through community practices. The way that communities practise shows their commitment to their negotiated values.

To develop this approach, certain conditions apply. People need to raise their own awareness of the significance of what they are doing as a form of social change, and have confidence in its legitimacy and importance. They also need to be aware of the politically constructed nature of the contexts in which they work. This means that they have to be aware of how powerful institutional voices have the capacity both to shut down their means of self-expression and avenues for the further development of their work and to support their efforts. This has major implications for those who are positioned as supporters to ensure that people are aware of the potential risks involved in undertaking their own enquiries, both in terms of the destabilisation that will happen in their own minds as a result of investigating their own potentials for knowing, and in terms of the potential backlash when they try to challenge the institutional power bases of established systems of knowledge. It is the responsibility of course providers to give emotional and practical support for people who are beginning to explore their thinking and imagining how they might change their own contexts. Providers need to enable practitioners to build up their intellectual self-defence, to see the potential retaliation for what it is, and to have courage not to submit, as well as develop their learning of how to deal with institutionalised power. They also need to encourage practitioners to build communities, so that they have support and comfort in times of difficulty, and find the inspiration to carry on.

None of this is easy. I say this from experience. It is, however, perfectly realisable, provided people have the energy and courage to commit to their own power as knowers, and to create their knowledge as it transforms into the creation of their lives.

Part II

What do we do?

The practices of action research

This section describes the practicalities of doing action research. Chapter 5 offers advice on how to conduct an action enquiry, and the case story by Siobhán Ní Mhurchú shows how the ideas can be implemented in practice. Chapter 6 gives advice on what to do and what not to do. Chapter 7 suggests how to make sense of the data, and Chapter 8 deals with issues of validating the data in support of claims to knowledge.

The section is written from my experience of doing action research. I offer advice as a research-active practitioner, from my experience of what works for me. You now have to try it out for yourself and generate your own testable ideas about what does and does not work for you, and then let other people know so that they can learn from you.

5 How to do action research

Planning and undertaking an action research project means asking questions about what we are doing, why, and how we can evaluate our practice in terms of the values we hold.

A practical guide to action research already exists in *You and Your Action Research Project* (McNiff *et al.*, 1996). I therefore do not intend to go into great detail here about how to do action research. In this book I want to present some key ideas, and also examples, to show how different people have approached their action enquiries, and how they have developed different insights into the process.

A basic action research process can be described as:

- We review our current practice,
- identify an aspect we want to improve,
- imagine a way forward,
- try it out, and
- take stock of what happens.
- We modify our plan in the light of what we have found and continue with the 'action',
- evaluate the modified action,
- and so on until we are satisfied with that aspect of our work.

(McNiff et al., 1996)

It is important, however, not to regard this as a rigid prescription of how things will turn out. It is idealised. Sometimes events do follow this sequence, as Siobhán's Ní Mhurchú's story in this chapter shows. Often, however, things do not turn out as we hope (see Chapter 10). Making sense of what happens when things do not go according to plan is just as much part of an action enquiry as when they do. The research is in the action, whether the action goes as we hope or not. The learning is in the practice.

It is also important to remember that, presented like this, elements of the model above appear as unproblematic. They can, however, be highly problematic. For example, 'identifying an aspect we want to improve' can be a very complex process. Sometimes we are not clear what it is we are trying to improve, or why.

Jack Whitehead regards the identification of a concern as methodologically central, because it raises the idea of the 'I' as a living contradiction. He says that the 'living I' should be placed at the centre of educational enquiries, not as an abstract personal pronoun but as a real-life human being. As a human being living and working in social contexts, 'I' often experience myself as a living contradiction in that I say one thing and do another. For example, I may believe in social democracy but do not always give people sufficient opportunity to state their point of view. Or I may feel that I should act in a particular direction but my work circumstances do not allow it. The contradiction can usually be understood in terms of how our values are denied in practice.

- I experience a concern when some of my educational values are denied in my practice;
- I imagine a solution to that concern;
- I act in the direction of the imagined solution;
- I evaluate the outcome of the solution;
- I modify my practice, plans and ideas in the light of the evaluation.

(Whitehead, 1989)

Similarly, imagining and implementing a possible solution can often be difficult, and we can spend time trying things out only to find they don't work. The experience, however, is all part of the learning, and time spent in trial and error is never wasted. The learning is what action research is all about.

Jack has further developed his ideas into an action plan:

- What is my concern?
- Why am I concerned?
- What do I think I can do about it?
- What will I do about it?
- How will I gather evidence to show that I am influencing the situation?
- How will I ensure that any judgements I make are reasonably fair and accurate?
- What will I do then?

In the next section Siobhán Ní Mhurchú, a member of the MA group in Cork, tells the story of her action research, which went fairly smoothly, so it is possible to see how she was able to implement her action plan, adapted from the above, in a coherent and systematic way. At other times, however, as Con Ó Muimhneacháin (Chapter 10), also in the Cork group, relates, the path is not so smooth. Sometimes it is not even possible to adopt a coherent strategy, as Kevin McDermott relates in Chapter 12. Kevin's focus is making sense of his own learning, and, while learning is definitely a practice, it is not always possible to adopt the systematic approach that Siobhán did.

Siobhán's story in many ways can be regarded as a 'classic' action research project. While it is in the context of mainstream education, the lessons travel equally to other work contexts.

HOW CAN I IMPROVE MY PRACTICE AS A TEACHER IN THE AREA OF ASSESSMENT THROUGH THE USE OF PORTFOLIOS?

Siobhán Ní Mhurchú

This account is a synopsis of the dissertation I wrote as part-fulfilment for my MA in education degree awarded by the University of the West of England, Bristol (Ní Mhurchú, 2000). I studied with a group of seven other colleagues, and Jean McNiff was our supervisor. You can access the whole dissertation on the website www.jeanmcniff.com. As a direct result of achieving my award, I am now appointed to work at national level with teachers of Irish as part of the inservice provision by the Irish Department of Education and Science for the New Curriculum, which began to be implemented in 2000.

My context

Until my secondment to Department of Education involvement this year I worked as a primary school teacher in County Waterford, Ireland. I began my MA studies in September 1998, and during these studies I encountered Howard Gardner's *Theory of Multiple Intelligences* (Gardner, 1983). I immediately saw the relevance of these ideas to my practice, and over time came to appreciate how I had placed a significant emphasis on logical and linguistic skills in my teaching, often to the detriment of other intelligences. I came to realise that I might have been condemning those students who did not excel in numerical and linguistic intelligence to a school life of boredom and frustration, and possibly denied them the opportunity to explore their other ways of knowing. This realisation acted as the spur to my enquiry. I resolved to find new ways of teaching which would recognise and value all forms of intelligence, and also develop new forms of assessment that supported learning, instead of the traditional punitive model which 'measured' only a narrow range of cognitive capacity.

During our study seminars I had heard a colleague, Con Ó Muimhneacháin (whose work appears in Chapter 10), speak with enthusiasm about his use of portfolios with students in secondary school. The more I heard him speak, the more I liked the idea. I felt this would work also in a primary school situation. It could become a new supplementary form of assessment in my classroom.

I was delighted to learn in 1999 that my plans were entirely in line with government recommendations as spelt out in the Introduction to the new curriculum (Government of Ireland, 1999b: 18):

> assessment is integral to all areas of the curriculum and it encompasses the diverse aspects of learning: the cognitive, the creative, the affective, the physical and the social . . . in order to take account of the breadth and variety of learning it offers, the curriculum contains a varied range of assessment tools. These range from informal tools such as teacher observation, class work, homework

and discussion with pupils to more formal tools such as diagnostic and standard-ised tests. Assessment tools such as projects, portfolios and curriculum profiles that can be used to link formal and informal approaches are also recommended.

I was therefore confident that my enquiry was addressing issues of concern not only to myself but also to policy-makers, and I began the project.

What was my concern?

I felt that I was denying my educational values in the area of assessment because I was using norm-referenced and standardised tests to judge the quality of the children's learning. I had believed I was doing a great job. I had worked hard to provide books that were of interest to students, and to ensure that each child could understand and apply each mathematical concept. I forgot, however, to see each child as an individual. I did not recognise the uniqueness of each child and the importance of their holistic development.

Why was I concerned?

At parent–teacher meetings in 1998 I used the results of norm-referenced tests in English and mathematics, Irish, geography, history and spelling to inform parents of their child's progress in school. I informed them of the position their child held in class as determined through these tests. I included no information on their child's ability in areas of physical education, art/crafts, music, and I made no reference to their interpersonal and intrapersonal capacities. I went home from those meetings with mixed emotions. I was disappointed at presenting my students' abilities as so many scores. This disappointment was compounded by the fact that I had been studying theories of multiple intelligences in my MA work, and I had been working very hard to try to move away from the traditional styles of learning and teaching, yet I seemed to be stuck with a narrow interpretation of intellectual capacity. I was labelling children according to their scores. My assessment methods lacked demo-cracy, justice, respect for others, freedom and individual integrity – all the values that mean so much to me in my personal and professional life. I was experiencing myself as a living contradiction (Whitehead, 1989), in that I held a set of values about the worth of each child yet I was systematically denying these values in my practice.

How could I present evidence to show the need to undertake the research?

In my dissertation appendices I have included the records which I used to inform parents at the parent–teacher meeting of October 1998. These records include norm-referenced tests in the subjects mentioned above. I have also included transcripts of conversations with my learning partner in the MA study group about my concerns.

What could I do?

First I needed to understand issues of assessment more fully, so I undertook substantial reading: Airasian (1996), Broadfoot (1979), Gipps (1994), Hyland (1998), Kingore (1993) and others. I kept records of the insights that were emerging from the reading, and how it was necessary, for example,

- to identify areas of learning difficulty;
- to record children's progress over time;
- to evaluate the suitability of the curriculum, resources, teaching methodologies;
- to support the process of teaching and learning.

I decided that I needed to find ways of developing forms of assessment that would identify individuals' strengths and aid their educational progress, a supportive rather than deficit model. I was already familiar with the processes of action research, since this was the underpinning philosophy of our MA studies and I had already done a piece of small-scale action research into my teaching of art (Ní Mhurchú, 1999), so it was self-evident to me that I would now undertake a planned action enquiry into how I could develop new forms of assessment in my classroom.

What did I do?

I continued to read in the areas of multiple intelligences and forms of assessment. I consulted with teacher colleagues about possible solutions to my concerns about how to develop a new method of assessment. While they were sympathetic and agreed with my thinking, they did not have any ideas for me, but they did reassure me that they would help in any way they could. I also began to pay particular attention to my colleague Con in the MA group who was using portfolios, and began to communicate regularly with him about how I might do the same.

I learnt from Con and also from my reading that portfolios deal with 'the individual's achievements relative to themselves rather than to others, and it looks for "best" rather than "typical" performances' (Gipps, 1994: 8). This method of assessment takes place in relatively uncontrolled conditions and any 'rules' are flexible. According to Pollard (1997: 303): 'To maximise the educational value, each child should be closely involved in the selection of evidence for inclusion in his or her portfolio, and in review of the contents.'

I identified a series of questions for myself in developing my ideas:

- What would the portfolios contain?
- Who would select the work?
- Why would students have portfolios?
- For whom is the assessment being done?

There was also a host of other questions, the answers to which at this point were a complete mystery. I was convinced, however, that this would be a great learning experience for me and would also be of benefit to my students.

I was at this stage acutely aware of the fact that undertaking the research meant critically reflecting on my own practice. I realised that I could not do this in isolation, and would need to involve colleagues, students and parents. I approached my principal to discuss the overall project. She was totally supportive.

I was aware of the need for good ethical practice and took pains to inform all participants and obtain permission to go ahead with my research.

I aimed to include all twenty-two students in fifth and sixth classes in my research (ages seven to eight), because I did not want to exclude anyone. I introduced the idea of portfolios into my classroom on 29 September 1999. I had read that the compilation of portfolios involved collection, selection, reflection and projection, and I resolved to work through these stages systematically with the children.

Collection

We discussed what the portfolios might contain – art/craft work, projects, tests, computer printouts, poems, lists of books they had read, and so on. I emphasised that it was important that what they selected should reflect some form of learning or understanding. I asked them to choose a day of the week which we could make our collection day, and they decided on Friday. We discussed how we would collect and store our materials. They chose cereal boxes as their portfolio containers and decorated the containers in their art class. The trouble was the boxes were bulky, but my principal offered to commission extra shelving for my classroom. During the course of the project, she became a regular visitor to our classroom to see how we were getting on and to wish us well.

Selection

The children wanted to get on immediately after the mid-term break. 'Can I put this medal I've won into my portfolio?' asked E on Monday morning. 'I think this is the best writing I've done in a long time,' said G. 'Can I put it in my portfolio?' Never let it be said that I dampened anyone's enthusiasm. I asked them to record the date on any item so that in later reviews the children themselves and any outside observer could see the learning progress over time.

Reflection

We encountered a huge difficulty here in that students found it hard to reflect on and evaluate their own work. I should have anticipated this. They were simply unfamiliar with the idea of self-assessment. They constantly came to me and asked if I thought this was 'good' or 'which do you think is better?' How could I help them to judge their own work? I suggested that they should ask themselves, 'Why did I choose this?' I really wanted them to become aware of their own strengths and abilities and come to appreciate how they were improving, or at least to find what needed working at in order to achieve their own identified standards.

I tried encouraging paired work and tape-recording so that they could talk through their ideas and also raise their sense of self-esteem, but their continuing difficulties with reflection and self-evaluation led to considerable doubts in my own mind. My journal of the time contains the comments 'What am I going to do? This is not working. Maybe portfolios and self-assessment are too difficult for primary school children.'

Kingore (1993) was helpful and lifted my spirits. He recommends that the teacher provide 'meaningful and appropriate guidance'. I decided that I should establish a set of criteria to help the children review their work and analyse its merits. I therefore drew up the following list of questions to help the children focus on developing their own criteria:

- What makes something your best work?
- How does this item show something important that you think or feel?
- How does this item show something that you have learnt?

Experience taught me to deal with one question per day, so Monday's question was: 'What makes this your best work?'

The responses were: 'Work we received a good grade in'; 'Work that was neat'; 'Something without mistakes'.

A key learning for us all happened when I asked them if their best work could include mistakes. They looked at their own and one another's work, and responded: 'If the work was difficult and you did your best' (student O); 'If it had improved on previous similar work' (student R). I was extremely pleased with these answers because I felt that their reflection on what is 'good' had moved on from believing that perfection was the only thing that was 'good'. I felt that these insights were particularly beneficial to less academic students who seemed to feel that they had little 'perfect' work to put into their portfolios. Now they could include work that, while less than 'perfect', was still good. This episode marked a development of understanding of the nature of self-evaluation both for the students and for me.

As time went on they learned to choose items which best represented their abilities, interests and accomplishments, and during this time I came to know more about each student. I also came to know a great deal more about myself.

The inclusion of out-of-school achievements

By late November children were beginning to produce items which departed from written representation. In October 1999 one of the students was chosen to take part in a children's television programme. This student's portfolio had been until now quite light because he does not excel in academic subjects, so you can imagine his pride and happiness on returning to school on 1 November with a video-recording of his debut on television to include in his portfolio. When he later completed a self-evaluation form on his use of his portfolio he wrote, 'This video is about my first time on TV. It is very hard to work on TV.' He claimed that 'my spellings have improved and my maths have also improved'. I like to think there is a correlation here, though it would be difficult to establish scientific grounds for this belief. I saw the difference in self-worth that the experience triggered, however.

At the end of each month we sifted through our work to pick the best efforts. Each student wrote an account, also for inclusion in the portfolio, about what their portfolio contained and what they were learning from the experience. I asked them to focus on the questions

- What is the best item in my portfolio this month?
- Why is it the best?
- What did I improve most in this month?
- Did I include anything different in my portfolio this month?
- What do I aim to improve next month?

After the Christmas holiday we put together their efforts from the previous three months and I hoped they would be able to trace improvement. I suggested they talk in threes or fours, to help them exchange opinion and learn from one another. Their comments included:

- 'Can we show them to other teachers?'
- 'Can we take them home to show our parents?'
- 'G read eighty-two books in three months! That's cool!'
- 'Can we do this for the rest of the year?'
- 'O has eight medals and three plaques. Wow!'

I was convinced that the portfolios demonstrated improved quality of work as well as developing insights into their own process of learning. I knew from our classroom interactions that they had helped one another to develop their learning. I needed to legitimate these feelings, and also produce evidence of the effectiveness of my approach in order to justify my change of practice and also to influence school policy in assessment, so I now focused on getting feedback from the students about their own experience of learning. It was difficult to find time to do this, but I scheduled two ten-minute slots per day within eleven days in January to meet with students individually to talk about their research. I tape-recorded our conversations. In hindsight I appreciate that I could have invited the students to make more class-room presentations of their work, and I will develop this idea in future research.

Here are some of the questions I asked each child:

- What would you like to show me first? Why?
- What's here that shows something important you have learnt?
- Can you show me something you can do now that you could not do before?
- At the end of November you felt you needed to improve in —. Has there been an improvement?
- What would you like to achieve by the next time we meet?

Involvement of parents

Students had the option in February of taking home their portfolios to share with their parents. I had written to parents previously to explain what we were doing, with a view to involving them in the assessment process. I asked parents to spend fifteen minutes with their child and to complete a review form about the experience. I hoped to shift parents' perceptions of their children's success, as my own perception had shifted, as being located in scores on a standardised test. I wanted parents to see their children as people of rich talent.

Parents' evaluation forms included the following (the standard questions on the form are in plain text, and parents' responses in italics):

- I want to thank *G* for sharing this portfolio with me.
- One of the aspects I especially enjoyed *was her fish bowl and the reading lists* because *it showed creativity and it showed the breadth of what the children can do.*
- What I liked about the whole portfolio *was the range of work being carried out is much greater than I thought – it is good to be made aware of this.*
- I think Scoil Gharbháin should continue to use this method of assessing the students because *it brings all the school activities home for everyone to see and it makes the students proud of their work.*

- I want to thank *O* for sharing this portfolio with me.
- One of the aspects I especially enjoyed was *O's artwork, and her pottery,* because *it really showed us her creative talent and her ability to be creative with clay.*
- What I liked about the whole portfolio was *it enables the parents but particularly the pupil to assess her development on a continuous basis, e.g. O's progress at maths.*
- I think Scoil Gharbháin should continue to use this method of assessing the students *because it certainly promotes an even greater enthusiasm and pride in their work and development.*

Projection

I wanted the students to look ahead and plan possible goals for the future. I asked them what areas they needed to concentrate on to improve their work. Each student identified specific areas. I like to think this demonstrated an increasing capacity to take responsibility for their own learning and how they were moving towards autonomy in creating their own futures.

What evidence could I produce to show how my actions were influencing my situation?

I collected a great deal of data during my project, not only the raw data relating to activities, but also reflective comments from a variety of sources. My data-gathering techniques included the following:

1   I systematically monitored my practice by keeping notes and daily records in my personal diary for the duration of the project. I recorded critical learning incidents throughout as well as my own reflection on my learning.

2   I made transcripts of tape-recorded interviews with the students.

3   I invited colleague S, the remedial teacher in school, to be my critical friend, and transcripts exist of interviews with her about the research. Her comments include: 'I believe that portfolios have transformed the learning environment in your classroom . . . You have also introduced the idea of self-assessment to them which makes them evaluate their own work and learning. You have taught them to look critically at their own work and helped them gauge what is good or what needs improving . . . Students have come to me speaking animatedly on something positive they have achieved . . . They have become their own teachers.'

4   One student took the initiative of making a tape-recording with his parents.

> *Student* Look, this is my best writing. Hasn't it improved.
> *Parent* Very good! I'm delighted to see the writing getting a little bigger.
> *Student* Here's an account of my football matches, my league matches, cup matches and what the score was that I played in. This is my book list from October.
> *Parent* How many books did you read? Fourteen books!
> *Student* And this is my list from November.
> *Parent* Very good. You're great for the books.

5   Students kept records of their own reflections of compiling their portfolios. I believe these clearly show the process of their own learning. They include:

- 'I wrote this play on my own and I am proud of it because not many children my age write plays.'
- 'My clay pot was the best thing that I did. I made it with my own hands. I painted it and glazed it myself. I think it is great.'
- 'I wrote this poem myself, and even though I entered a competition I didn't win but I am proud.'
- 'It was the first time I won two plaques in a row. I won these plaques for Irish dancing.'
- 'My spellings have really improved this year. My maths has improved too.'
- 'I won four medals for musician of the week because I practised every night.'
- 'Within a period of three months I read eighty-two books. Even I surprised myself.'

6   Colleague R visited my classroom to attend the presentation of portfolios by the children to their peers. His report includes these comments: 'What was abundantly clear was the pride that each child displayed regarding his/her own portfolio. It seemed as if the contents represented a personal treasure chest

of achievements . . . It was clear that children were very much involved in choosing what went into their own portfolio and therefore felt a personal responsibility and ownership of its contents . . . Some individuals did seem to be moving closer to a greater degree of personal analysis of their progress . . . The improvement in their work over time was apparent to every child and it seemed that their portfolios were instrumental in informing them of this . . . The overall impression I felt in the classroom from the children was a positive awareness of their own learning and a feeling of empowerment to improve their learning.'

7 I have samples of portfolios which students allowed me to hold until September 2000 when they will be returned, according to Bassey's (1999) guidelines regarding storage of data.

8 Response sheets were returned from all parents as completed on the evening when their child made their portfolio presentation in the home. There is no negative comment anywhere. These sheets are stored in my archive.

9 I took photographs of the students sifting through their portfolios for their 'best work'. The expressions of joy and enthusiasm on their faces are evident (see colleagues' comments below, p.82).

10 I made a presentation on our staff planning day of a student's portfolio. This day was part of the Department of Education and Science inservice provision in preparation for the introduction of the new curriculum. Colleague R reports on my presentation thus: 'Many of the other teachers . . . following a presentation given by Siobhán at a staff planning day are trying out this use of authentic assessment. We were very impressed by the examples of the portfolios we were shown as well as by Siobhán's enthusiasm for the project. She has pushed the staff to see beyond the usual areas of assessment when appraising the children in their care.'

I believe, from the above, that I am justified in claiming that:

- the students became more involved in their own assessment;
- I as their teacher had afforded them more learning opportunities;
- their motivation to learn and improve their work had increased;
- I had made my colleagues more aware of a means of assessment which included a wide range of abilities across all the subjects of the curriculum.

What conclusions did I draw from my evidence? How did I judge my own effectiveness?

I believe that I have shown how the introduction of portfolio work contributed to an enhanced learning experience for the students and for myself. Through my research I was able to evaluate the learning and understanding that had taken place, and I believe I encouraged the students to develop the capacity also to reflect critically on their own work, make decisions how to improve it, and show their reasons and intentions for so doing. In other words, I think I enabled my students to carry out their own action research into their practice and develop confidence in their capacity to reflect critically on this process.

For myself, I have moved from a position of judging my work in terms of testing and technical achievement to assessing it as a form of praxis. I judge my practice in terms of whether I am fulfilling my values of democracy, justice, individual autonomy and collaborative learning. I think all these aspects are evident in my work as it impacts on the quality of learning of the children.

How did I show that I took care that my judgements were reasonably fair and accurate?

From the beginning of my research I set up validation groups – one comprising my students as research participants, and another comprising a colleague, and a critical friend. Later the principal of the school and two other colleagues expressed an interest in developments, and offered their support in commenting on the progress of my research. I did not initially consider involving parents formally in the validation process, but over time I came to see that their informal feedback was a vital aspect of supporting my claims to have improved my work. In future work I will ensure that a parent becomes part of a formal validation group. My MA group always acted as another source of critical appraisal and encouragement, and we used some of our seminar times to comment on one another's work. As they viewed the photographs, colleagues said: 'They say they are improving in spelling and maths and they are pointing to the evidence in their portfolios. That's evidence of personal awareness of learning'; 'Look at how they are interacting. They are obviously enjoying working together.'

How did I modify my practice?

I am aware of the following changes in my own teaching:

*   I introduced the children to a method of assessment which gave them an opportunity to show what they know, what they have learnt, what they can do, and how they understand their own process of learning.
*   I gave them an opportunity to celebrate their success as learners rather than stay with a system which emphasised error, failure and inadequacy.
*   I involved them in their own learning and assessment of their learning.
*   I introduced a collaborative assessment approach involving students, teachers and parents.
*   I introduced the idea to my colleagues. The staff seemed impressed. One teacher commented, 'Very few educational innovations could make such broad claims.' Portfolios have been welcomed as part of the school policy of assessment from 14 February 2000.

Conclusion

My dissertation reflects the changing nature of my work in school and my role as a teacher–researcher. It offers an understanding of professional development that took place in a school and is directly related to the learning of the pupils and the people within it. I can make my claims to knowledge because with the support of participants I can show that I have improved my work and explain how and why I have done so. I can show how knowledge can assume a living form through the processes of reformulation and reworking.

The research has raised interesting new questions for me, such as

- Can one form of assessment be relied upon or should a judicious balance of approaches be employed over time?
- If portfolio work cannot tell where the student stands in relation to a class average, or to a national norm, will standardised tests be used for that purpose?
- If the public is demanding accountability should this be judged only in terms of standardised testing?

These questions become the beginning of new action enquiries. Now that I am on my learning journey, there is no stopping.

Significance of the research

For me

I believe that I have achieved what I set out to do which was to improve the quality of learning experience for my students through critically reflecting on my own practice and how I could improve it. I have focused on my values and examined my classroom practice in the light of those values. I have revealed the nature of my values as the living standards of judgement I used in making sense of and explaining my educational development (Whitehead, 1993, 2000). In writing this report I believe I am showing what research-based professionalism means for education.

I am now clearer about my own potential, the positive power of believing in my own capacity to improve the quality of my life, and I think I have transferred this assurance to the students. They are now able formally to celebrate their value as human beings.

The writing up of the dissertation has been significant in helping me to understand my own educational development. I believe I have developed my own living educational theory (Whitehead, 1989) and I have moved beyond depending on the theories of others.

For my workplace

Colleagues have expressed an interest in learning from my research. They have monitored my work and assessed its effectiveness for themselves on the basis of the evidence I have produced. In February 2000 the school adopted portfolio assessment as school policy.

I believe that if you can give people hope when dealing with a particular problem, if you can show them a practical way, the problem can be overcome from within people's own resources. I would like to see the staff's experience of coming to understand the usefulness of my research extended to national policy. If action research were adopted as a form of professional development on a national scale, teachers' self-perceptions would rise and we would be looking at an invigorated workforce that had the confidence to take an active role in improving society. I believe that action research might be a more viable option for the Department of Education and Science in supporting professional development as it taps into a source of energy and goodwill that would enable people to innovate and manage change for themselves in their own educational environments. The introduction of the new curriculum is a golden opportunity to explore the potential of this form of professional education.

For education

I believe that I have contributed to new forms of educational research and theory. I have shown how I have generated my own theories out of my practice, and how the theories themselves are part of the practice of ongoing modification and improvement.

I have come to understand that I can contribute to a much wider body of knowledge. This report is part of that body of knowledge which is transforming what the research community understands as legitimate theory. As I have influenced the quality of professional learning in my classroom and my workplace, so I hope also to influence the wider community of researchers in their understanding of how knowledge is produced and used within practitioners' individual and collective practices. I have become aware of my own potential for influence, both in local and wider contexts, and I intend to take every opportunity to share my learning in my hope for a more democratic and caring approach to education in schools.

6 Practical issues

Action research is practical. Here is some advice on what to do and what not to do.

Stay small, stay focused

There can be a big difference between the scope of your work and the scope of your action research project. Even though the area may not be small, the study itself should focus on one aspect of the overall picture so that it is always clear what you are researching. Although, in a wide sense, work and practice are research, and research is practice, in a practical sense you need to see your project as an extrapolation from your wider work and keep it in perspective.

You are researching you, so one piece of your practice is probably going to be symptomatic of the whole. You could find that researching one aspect will reveal other interconnected aspects – you and your work are synthesised and everything is interconnected and mutually influential. Don't try to research everything at once, though. You need to stay focused on one issue, and get on the inside of it and understand it, and put the others on hold. Concentrating on only one part of your work helps you to understand the nature and process of your own learning. Once you have come to a point where you feel you have made progress in one aspect (you will probably not bring anything to closure but you will move to a new place in your understanding), you can then progress to other areas which themselves will become new research projects.

Identify a clear research question

You need to be reasonably clear about what you are researching. Action research asks a question of the kind, 'How do I . . .?' For example, 'How do I improve the quality of my relationship with X?' 'How do I help Y to learn more effectively?' 'How do I manage my time more efficiently?' These questions emphasise that you are at the centre of the research. This does not mean that you are working in isolation; you are always in relation with others, and you will check whether you are making progress by seeking feedback from those others, and also evaluating whether you are influencing them so that their own learning is advanced.

As an action researcher you would not ask questions of the kind, 'How many people have achieved a specified level of expertise?' 'What do other people say about this event?' 'Is there a relationship between room temperature and degree of concentration?' These kinds of question belong to an empirical approach, where the aim is to establish facts and figures and check the viability of hypotheses. Action researchers recognise the validity of these approaches, and are interested in questions which produce answers about quantity, but they are more interested in quality and how they can ensure quality by studying their own practice. They see factual issues as embedded within wider issues to do with the quality of experience.

Be aware that the research question might change as you develop the research. The question 'How do I help my students concentrate?' might transform into the question 'How do I make my lessons more interesting so that my students want to learn?' As you reveal issues through studying your practice you will come to new understandings about yourself and the problematics of your situation and begin asking new questions.

Be realistic about what you can do; also be aware that wider change begins with you

Can you do anything about the unsatisfactory superstructure of your organisation? Possibly not immediately. It is difficult to nurture sustainable change from the outside, more feasible from within. You can, however, certainly change wider systems by focusing on and improving a smaller piece within the system, as a participant. You can understand and modify the piece of the infrastructure which constitutes you working with others, and you can influence others on an increasingly wider scale by producing accounts of your work and showing how that is beneficial to others in other contexts. You cannot change the world immediately, but you can change your piece of it, and you can influence others to change theirs. This is a powerful methodology for social change. It is a process of individuals deciding that they want to change their own lives and then coming together as communities of like-minded practitioners who mobilise themselves for action. Change begins in individuals' minds; it develops by individuals talking with one another and taking action as a result of their collective decisions. It is long term, labour intensive, resilient to opposition, and a powerful force which should not be underestimated.

Plan carefully

This means having a broad outline of where you hope the research will lead but it does not mean setting specific objectives. Often the research will develop in ways different to what you had expected, and you might need to shift the focus and change the research question. From the beginning set yourself working criteria about how you are going to judge your effectiveness. You might need to modify and refine your criteria as you go. If, for example, you were trying to help X improve their confidence, you might set a criterion such as 'Did X smile?' or 'Did X challenge someone's opinion in a meeting?' In your records you would have noted instances when, before you began working with X, they never smiled or challenged an opinion. As you worked away and monitored your practice you would gather data, a photograph perhaps, where X smiled, or make a note in your journal that X challenged an opinion.

Criteria are linked to our values. If we choose the criteria 'X smiled' or 'X challenged an opinion' to test whether we are being effective in our work, we hold values around the need for people to feel happy and confident, to exercise their freedom of mind and action. Our values inform our work, and our work can be judged in terms of whether we are living our values in our practice.

Set a realistic timescale

The wider project that is your lifework goes on. The specific project you are working on is bounded. Aim to set time limits, but realistic enough to cope with unpredictability. It is useful to set two time limits: first, an ideal which you might potentially achieve; and a second more generous limit which you must achieve. You need to show others that you are managing your project appropriately. If you have set deadlines, perhaps for people to return an edited transcript, ensure also that you honour commitments. It is important to maintain credibility, not only for yourself, but for the knowledge base that you stand for.

Involve others

As a social being, you are always in company with others. They might not be present, but you and they are still influencing one another. Action research is always research with, not research on (Rowan and Reason, 1981).

You are inevitably involved with others in doing your research in the following ways.

As research participants

You will invite others whose situation you are trying to improve or whose learning you are trying to nurture to be research participants. If you are exploring how you can increase the degree of workplace participation in decision-making, you will monitor how your actions impact on others. This involves you getting feedback from them as to how well you are helping them to help themselves. While the research focus is you and your learning you are also understanding how your learning is influencing the quality of learning of others.

As observers

Be public about your research so that it does not appear mysterious. Invite others to observe you and ask for their feedback. At a public relations level others will warm to you; at a research level you are showing that your research is rooted in an ethic of respect for others' opinions.

As validators

Submit your research and its findings for critical scrutiny to ensure that any conclusions you might come to are not just your own opinion but are agreed by others. It might be that your ideas have come in for critique. Colleagues might have made suggestions about how you should revise your research and your ideas. When you produce your report, aim to build in these factors, and show how you took action on the advice of others to help you think or act more purposefully.

As potential researchers

As a real-world researcher you are inevitably involved in wider systemic change. You are part of a living system with others; you are studying how you can improve your own work which involves others; you are investigating how you can influence and encourage them to investigate how they can do the same. You are encouraging them to regard their practice as research, and you are establishing communities of action researchers who are studying how they can improve their learning for mutual benefit.

Ensure good ethical practice

Be aware of your own potential abuse of position power. People often become enthused by the idea that they can create their own futures, and there is a danger that people might use their enthusiasm to serve their own purposes. Have you heard the Marx Brothers' joke that once you get the sincerity right everything else will follow? It is difficult to judge the authenticity of someone else's mission; a lot of faith is involved. Habermas (1979) is probably right when he says that we judge over time whether people are engaging, or only pretending to engage, in communicative action.

There are other widely accepted aspects of doing ethically informed research (see, for example, Robson, 1993). They include:

- negotiate access
  - with authorities
  - with participants
  - with parents, guardians and supervisors
- promise confidentiality
  - of information
  - of identity
  - of data
- ensure participants' rights to withdraw from the research
- keep others informed
- maintain your own intellectual property rights
- keep good faith

(See McNiff *et al.*, 1996: 34–5.)

Concentrate on learning, not on the outcomes of action

It is tempting to focus on activity only and to produce a report that offers descriptions of the activity – what you did and how you did it. This descriptive level is important but insufficient. It stays at the level of E-theorising. To move to I-theorising, aim to show the process of learning that informed the activities, why you did what you did, and what you hoped to achieve.

In doing the research and in producing the report think in terms of two complementary processes. One process is to do with your activity with others. The other is to do with your learning with others. The way we develop our learning with others influences the way we develop our actions.

Think about how you understand what you are doing (your practice) and how you can develop it in new, better ways. You are considering the reasons and purposes of your research, how you are reflecting critically on your own learning, and offering an explanation for your practice. Think about the actions you took to implement your ideas and to test their effectiveness by gathering, presenting and interpreting data, and how those actions influenced and inspired the actions of others. The two processes of action and reflection are inextricably linked and mutually influential. The learning influences the action and the action influences the learning. Theory and practice are interdependent. The theory turns into practice and practice becomes theory. Theory is the lived practice, integrated within the life of the practitioner.

The focus of the research is you, in company with others

In interpretative action research, researchers observe others doing their action research, and offer accounts of activities. Researchers speak on behalf of others. In self-study, researchers observe themselves. They speak on their own behalf and encourage others to do the same. The communities they form are composed of autonomous people, independent in mind and action, who are committed to accepting the responsibility of their own actions and potential influence.

In living theory approaches researchers focus on themselves and their own learning. They recognise that they are always in company with others, so reflecting on one's practice means reflecting on how one is with others. Because action research has educational intent, reflecting on one's own practice with others means investigating how one can ensure that the practice is educational, that is, mutually beneficial and life affirming to all parties. In undertaking an action enquiry a researcher is investigating how they can improve their own learning so that they are better placed to help others.

It is tempting only to observe and describe what other people are doing. This is the dominant view in the social sciences. To ensure that action research is an educative practice it is essential to remember that 'I' have to remain at the centre of the enquiry as a potential influence for good in the lives of others. The I-theories that 'I' generate show how and why I am accepting responsibility for my own thoughts and actions.

Beware of happy endings

A widespread mythology is that life episodes have happy endings. This is seldom the case. Life is full of problematics. Utopia exists only in the imagination (thankfully so, because the conformity of harmony would be suffocating for many). The struggle to create a good society, however, is real. Through our struggles we each take incremental steps which bring us closer to where we want to be. Bell *et al.* (1990) explain the process, when commenting on the work of Horton and Freire, as creating the road by walking it. We also need to be aware that in the creative process we are changing our own present realities so that our vision of where we want to be is also changing. Insofar as the future is in the present, we create the future as we change the present. We are not aiming for happy endings so much as good present situations.

Action researchers do not aim for closure in which notionally unsatisfactory situations transform into satisfactory ones. They start from where they are, albeit with a sense that something needs doing, even if that something is thinking carefully about where they are. They take action to evaluate whether what they are doing is the best it can be, and how they can improve it where necessary. This often leads to some improvement but not perfection (see Siobhán Ní Mhurchú's idea in Chapter 5 that good work does not mean perfect work). It is important, however, to monitor and explain the process of learning. Learning from processes where things do not go right is as valuable as when they do. The struggle to make sense is the research process. It does not matter that an external situation does not go as one hopes. What is important is to be aware of the problematics, to use these as rich opportunities for learning, and to explain the process so that others can learn from the account. In fact, it is well to be cautious when things do seem to be going smoothly. Are you overlooking problematics which, while potentially disturbing, indicate that perhaps interesting issues should be explored?

Be aware of political issues

Action research is always political, because an aim is to influence people to change their situations. Many people feel comfortable with the status quo, possibly because it is familiar. They might complain about where they are but familiarity gives security and it is difficult for many to break the emotional bonds, even if they know at a cognitive level that they should. Other people are comfortable with the status quo because it suits them, particularly if they have a position of power and are unwilling to encourage public participation in decision-making.

Action researchers are beset by these kinds of external circumstance, as well as the accompanying problematics of resources and support. They are also beset by their own internal constraints of lack of confidence, or their capacity to take action, or the possible challenge from colleagues. Undertaking self-study to see how one can recreate oneself in order to help others to recreate themselves is far from straightforward, and many people, sadly but understandably, give up the struggle as the pressures begin to bite.

We all make our own decisions about who we are and who we want to be, and, as far as we are able, we make our own decisions about what we intend to do.

7 Making sense of the data and generating evidence

This chapter talks about gathering, presenting and interpreting data, and generating evidence to support a claim to knowledge. Chapter 8 deals with validating claims to knowledge.

In action research terms data refers to information. We systematically monitor what we are doing in order to gather information about it. We organise the data in a variety of ways, reflect on it, draw conclusions from it, and present those conclusions with the data for the critical scrutiny of others. We aim to make an original claim to knowledge, that is, to say that we know something which was not known before. To ensure that the claim is not seen only as our own opinion we have to support the claim with validated evidence, drawn from the data.

This chapter considers how to make sense of the data using an action–reflection cycle as an organising framework: identify a concern, imagine a solution, implement the solution, observe the influence, evaluate the outcomes, modify actions and ideas in the light of the evaluation, plan for the next step. The framework gives us a series of questions:

- What is my concern? Which issue am I attending to? Can I gather information about it?
- What solutions can I imagine? How am I going to gather the data? Which techniques can I use?
- How can I implement the solution? How do I monitor the action? How do I observe and describe what is happening?
- How will I evaluate the solution? How will I make sense of the data in terms of success criteria? What will my claim to knowledge look like?
- How will I modify my actions and ideas in the light of the evaluation? How will I practise in order to influence others and our situations?

What is my concern?

Which issue do I want to look at? What research question will I ask?

Identifying a research focus also implies formulating a research question. Action research questions are of the 'How do I . . .?' kind. Often the question takes the form 'How do I improve . . .?', and the research focus is something in your situation which you feel you can do something about.

It is important to bear in mind which areas do and do not lend themselves to action research questions. Generally speaking, action research approaches are appropriate for issues to do with values and how these values can be realised in practice. They are not appropriate for issues which aim, for example, to show the relationship between variables.

Action research approaches are appropriate for issues such as:

- I would like to improve the quality of relationships in my workplace. What can I do?
- I would like to introduce ICT into my classrooms. How can I show the link between ICT and the quality of learning?
- Why the low take-up for the annual party?
- How can I arrange for the freer dissemination of ideas among the staff?

Action research approaches are not appropriate for issues such as:

- What is the link between children's socio-economic status and their enjoyment of literature?
- What do people think about the president?
- How does management style relate to productivity?
- How many customers visit the store on Saturday morning?

Having mapped out what you want to investigate, it is important to focus on one aspect that you feel you can do something about. Be aware, however, that the focus of the research might change and be refined, and the research question with it. Although you would begin with a general sense of a particular issue, sometimes the focus only emerges over time. You might begin by asking, 'How can I improve the quality of staff relationships?' and find that your question changes to, 'How can I improve my management style in order to improve the quality of staff relationships?'

Beginning action research also involves making decisions about what you can and cannot do, given the situation in which you are working. In their *Action Research Planner*, Kemmis and McTaggart (1988) emphasise that beginning an action research project involves strategic planning and recognition of the social conditions which have possibly inspired you to become active. Intervening involves not only an initial question – 'What is to be done?' – but also the strategic question 'What can be done?' It involves recognising limitations as well as potentialities.

> What can be done in your situation will be limited. You cannot sweep away the world which currently exists in your school, classroom or community; you may challenge its character and boundaries, but to change it you must recognise what it is now, and where you can work to change it. Deciding where to begin is a *strategic decision* – it is a practical decision about where to act

to produce *the most powerful effect compatible with sustaining the struggle of reform.*

(Kemmis and McTaggart, 1988: 65; emphasis in original)

What solutions can I imagine?

How am I going to gather the data? Which techniques can I use?

You will find, especially in the early stages of the project, that you will gather quantities of data, much of which will later be discarded. At the beginning, however, it is important not to reject anything that might count later as valuable data.

Data-collection techniques fall into three broad categories: paper and pen techniques, live techniques and ostensive techniques. (A considerable literature exists about how to gather data, and new texts are appearing which deal with new forms of data: see, for example, Prosser, 1998).

Paper and pen

These include the following.

Field notes

You would keep notes of the situation 'in the field' as important instances of critical incidents. The field can be a workplace, a bus queue, a classroom, a home. You will aim to document significant aspects of the action: for example, two colleagues had a difference of opinion today, so you set up a mediating strategy to avoid further confrontation. Both left the meeting still aggrieved but at least prepared not to make a wider issue of it.

Diaries and logs

You would aim to keep your own diary, and also encourage other research participants to do so. It is useful to divide your diary into two columns headed 'What I did' (or 'action' or another term to show that you are describing the action) and 'What I learned' (or 'reflection' or another term to show that you are reflecting on the action). It is easy enough to describe what happened; showing the learning is more difficult, but it is essential.

If you invite other research participants to keep diaries, reassure them that their diaries are confidential. They do not have to make their diaries available to you, although clearly these are rich sources of data. You need to negotiate these matters as part of the research.

Diaries are particularly valuable sources of data because they show not only a development in the action but also a development in thinking. You can document how your own perceptions changed over time, and show how you used new learning to help make better sense of a situation.

Reports

Reports can exist in a variety of forms: accounts, letters, memos. If you wanted to find out what people felt about a situation you might ask them to write you a letter to describe how they saw the situation and how they felt about it. This takes courage because you are exposing your own vulnerability to others. What will you do if you receive letters suggesting that you have to change your own ways? Are you prepared for your own possible reaction?

Building up an archive of reports over time can help you to keep track of the action, your own and other people's, and see how issues and opinions changed over time.

Questionnaires

Use these only if you must. Questionnaires are helpful but notoriously difficult to construct. They are also liable to misuse.

In action research you might want to use questionnaires to get an idea of trends. Further detailed analysis of the data is often necessary using more qualitative forms which aim to see whether values are being lived in practice. Open-ended questions can provide richer data than closed questions, but analysing the responses is more labour and time intensive.

Live

These include the following.

Sociometric methods

These are much used in sociological analysis, where social relationships are captured using diagrams to show interactions.

It is, however, important not to draw rigid conclusions from such diagrams. They might provide initial information and perhaps an incentive for you to investigate the situation further. They should not be taken as the way things always are. In Figure 7.1 A–E represent people and the hashes on each line represent the number

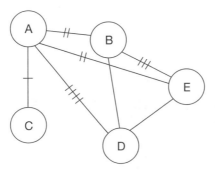

Figure 7.1 Sociometric analysis

of interactions between them. The isolate at C might be feeling unwell on the day you do the observation; normally they might be the most outgoing of the group. While useful, these snapshots are still synoptic illusions.

Interviews and discussions

These are valuable sources of data and capture the lived response of people to the situation. They are time and labour intensive. You would need to do some analysis of the discussion to indicate trends, as well as draw up a report to show general conclusions. It would probably be best to tape-record conversations, but then you have to do some transcribing (see also next section).

In interviews it is best to adopt an open-ended approach, otherwise it would be as sensible to use a questionnaire. Interviews always need to be conducted with care and consideration for the interviewee, and it is important to refine your own interviewing and counselling skills if you are using this method.

Ostensive

Stills presentations

These include slide/tape presentations, and the use of software packages such as PowerPoint. While they can be attractive they can also be limiting in what they portray. If you are hoping to show participants' actions through photographs, remember that the photos will portray abstracted pieces of action which need to be contextualised by other means. Photographs and commentaries can be very useful to show changes in actions but not changes in attitudes (see Schratz, 1998, and Schratz and Steiner-Löffler, 1998, for helpful ideas on the use of photographs in practitioner research).

Audiotaped interviews

One of the best data-gathering techniques, audiotape, however, has drawbacks in terms of the amount of effort you have to put in to get what you are looking for. Tapes must be transcribed in whole or part, and transcribing is a very lengthy business. You should aim to present the tape itself (probably in your archive or the appendix) along with the transcript, in whole or part, when you submit your report.

Videotape

This includes use of other technology such as digital cameras. This is the most powerful medium yet available to show the reality of situations. It is possible to show the nuances of the action to communicate how values are being lived in practice. Many accrediting institutions now accept multimedia presentations as part of action research reports. It is possible, for example, using packages such as Hypertext, for the researcher to appear on screen commenting on the process of what is happening at another place on the screen (see Chapter 8 for further discussion).

Remember with all live and ostensive methods that it is very important to get permission from participants to be on tape. This is particularly important when working with children, and is a pertinent issue in these days of freedom of information and potential litigation.

How can I implement the solution?

How do I monitor the action? How do I observe and describe what is happening?

Monitoring the action means monitoring the practice of yourself, and of others as your own practice impacts on them. Remember that you are not researching other people. You are researching yourself, but that involves how you are influencing others.

Monitoring your own action

This involves keeping records of your own thoughts and actions as they relate to your original intentions and purposes. Are you achieving what you set out to do? Do you need to act in different ways? Monitoring the action is part of evaluating it.

You can do this by keeping a research diary. Systematically write up your activities and reflections. Note any shifts in emphasis.

You can also generate data by inviting others to monitor your actions. This might take the form of written or oral feedback, or you could invite a colleague to observe you and offer feedback. At this point it is worthwhile involving your critical friend or validation group to look at your data and make suggestions about how you could interpret it or modify your actions.

Monitoring other people's action

Other people become participants in your research. You can monitor their actions and thoughts by inviting them to keep research diaries themselves which they could make available to you. If you were investigating an issue directly concerning someone else, such as how you could improve the quality of learning for students, you could monitor the students' learning to see whether you were making the impact you wish. Remember that you need to get permission beforehand to monitor other people. This applies particularly when the other people are vulnerable, such as children.

When you monitor others, or invite them to monitor themselves, you need to check that all accounts are reasonably in agreement. Triangulation is helpful here, when the data is scrutinised from multiple perspectives in order to reach reasonable agreement that the situation is as you say it is.

Sorting the data

It is also important to start sorting your data as soon as you can. This will help you to make sense of the project in an ongoing way. Decide first on initial categories, and sort the data into these categories. As you go on you might want to devise new categories.

How will I evaluate the solution?

How will I make sense of the data in terms of criteria? What will my claim to knowledge look like?

We usually judge success in terms of criteria. The proof of the pudding is in the eating (in action research terms the word 'proof' seldom appears; we can hope only to provide evidence to support a reasonable claim that something is effective).

The criteria we set to judge success relate to our values. For example, if we are hoping to develop good working relationships among the staff, we hold a value that productive work is rooted in good relationships where everyone feels valued and respected. We can identify criteria, such as 'Do colleagues feel valued and respected?' The criteria can be refined and focused in terms of behaviours and attitudes: 'Does Mr M speak more in staff meetings? Does Ms B speak more positively than before?' In your action research you are hoping to show your influence in other people's lives. Can you show that Mr M became more confident, and Ms B became more positive because of your influence? You need to show the line of influence between what you believe in and whether these values had an influence for good in other people's lives.

If you feel that you have developed your understanding of practice, and possibly improved a situation, you would be entitled to say so, provided you can support that claim with validated evidence. Your right to make a claim to knowledge revolves around whether you feel you know something that you did not know before, and can validate that knowledge. The knowledge may not be new for someone else, but it is new knowledge for you. Polanyi (1967) says that every time someone says, 'I know that . . .', they are adding to the existing store of knowledge. You are contributing to the wider body of knowledge when you say, 'I understand my work better than I did before' (in the wider theoretical terms of this book, when you can produce your own I-theory).

However, our theories remain so much speculation unless we support them with evidence which has been validated by others. Throughout your project you should aim to involve others as critical friends and validators. You should aim to convene a validation group at critical points throughout your research to scrutinise your data, listen to your findings, and agree (or not) that you have a right to make your claim to knowledge. They will also make suggestions about how you might refine your work or make it more rigorous. This focus on the need for methodological rigour has developed over recent years, and enables action research to be seen as a well-formed discipline of education.

How will I modify my actions and ideas in the light of the evaluation?

How will I practise in order to influence others and our situations?

Further action–reflection cycles will incorporate the insights developed in earlier ones. Having learnt how to help Mr M raise his level of confidence you can now use the learning to help others.

Remember now what you are doing at a wider level. While you are aiming initially to improve your understanding in order to improve a local situation, your wider commitment is towards creating good social orders in which all are committed to improving their practice for mutual benefit. This means that you have to encourage others to see the potential value of studying their own practice to help one another.

Your action research could therefore begin to take on a wider social perspective. Can you now produce evidence to show how you are influencing others to develop their collective learning and improve organisational and social settings? Can you show how you are influencing others to undertake their own action enquiries in their own practices and how those enquiries are also mutually beneficial? Can you show how your I-enquiry influenced others to undertake theirs, so that multiple I-enquiries then become C-enquiries (community, collective enquiries), and how this developed focus then moved communities towards a better life for all? These generative transformational processes need careful nurturing by people positioned as educational leaders, and accounts are already appearing to show the process and its benefits (for example, Dodd, 2001; Nugent, 2000; Roche, 2000).

An example of making sense of the data and generating evidence

Making sense of the data means we are generating evidence to support a claim to knowledge.

Let's say that Mary is a course leader on a management course. A participant in the group, Mr J, is reluctant to contribute to the sessions. He sits there silently, and when invited to speak appears uncomfortable. Mary wonders how she can encourage Mr J to contribute. She believes that he lacks self-confidence.

Mary's concern is to encourage Mr J to contribute to the session.

The reasons she feels it is important to encourage Mr J to contribute include the value that she puts on participation. She feels that all members of a group should believe that their contributions are valued. If people do not feel confident about themselves and their opinions, they will probably not wish to contribute. Besides, in his position as a manager, Mr J will need to have confidence in himself in order to inspire confidence in others.

Mary decides that she will help Mr J to raise his self-confidence. She will do this through encouragement, finding ways to involve Mr J without making him feel vulnerable. How to involve him without making him feel vulnerable becomes Mary's research focus. Mary thinks that she will be able to say she has succeeded in finding ways to help Mr J feel confident if Mr J begins to behave in ways that demonstrate self-confidence. She will judge her own practice in the light of Mr J's practice as a response to her own.

She initially gathers data both about her own behaviour as well as Mr J's. So that he is fully aware of what she is doing, she invites him to help her monitor her own work as a course leader. She asks him to keep a diary in which he records what Mary did and how he felt about this. Mr J is happy to support Mary in her work. The data-gathering techniques she uses are her own diary, Mr J's diary (he has given her permission to use it), field notes and observations.

Mary sets herself criteria by which she is going to judge her effectiveness. As noted above, her effectiveness can be assessed in terms of Mr J's behaviour. Did he become more confident? How did he manifest this? Mary decides on three simple criteria:

- Did Mr J smile at people more than before?
- Did he offer an opinion during a group discussion?
- Did he challenge an opinion and offer an alternative point of view?

Mary feels that these criteria would signal improved self-confidence.

The way that Mary tries to involve Mr J without making him feel vulnerable is to praise him in a discreet way; she avoids using hard phrases such as 'No' and 'I don't think so'; she is empathetic throughout; she generates an atmosphere of care among the group by listening carefully to everyone and encouraging everyone to do the same; she smiles and nods frequently; she always includes Mr J in group activities; she arranges for pair work so that people will not be exposed to the larger group discussion until they feel ready for it; and so on. In short, Mary practises a combination of counselling skills, listening skills and general good facilitation practices.

Mary continues to monitor her own practice and gather data over a period of three weeks. Mr J maintains his diary throughout. At intervals Mary checks her data to see whether she can find any instances of the criteria in action. This means that she sorts the data, and sifts through it to find instances of whether he smiled more, offered an opinion, or challenged an opinion and offered an alternative point of view. Among the considerable quantity and wide variety of data she finds two instances only: a note jotted in her field book when she wrote, 'Mr J seemed in a very good mood today. He was smiling at everyone!'; and in her diary the comment, 'Mr J disagreed with Mrs X today, very mildly, but he did disagree.' These instances act as evidence, the realisation of our values in practice. Evidence is not data; it is drawn from the data. Data transforms into evidence when actions show that the criteria we have set ourselves are realised. Mary decides not to throw out the rest of the data, because other aspects might be revealed as important as the research progresses and possibly the focus shifts.

Feeling that she is making progress, Mary asks the group if they would agree to her videotaping herself in company with them. Everyone agrees. When she later comes to look at the videotape with the group, she notes that Mr J took a lively interest in the proceedings, and offered an opinion on several occasions. Mary believes that this shows that Mr J is raising his level of self-confidence, so Mary can say that she has improved her practice through the evidence of Mr J's improved self-confidence.

To ensure that her claim is not regarded only as her opinion, Mary invites the group to comment on her work, and she invites Mr J to say whether he feels that he is contributing more. He speaks at length about how he feels at ease with the group. Mary asks and receives the group's permission to show the videotape to her research validation group. The validation group agrees that Mary has developed useful facilitation skills which have possibly influenced Mr J's behaviour and attitudes. They agree that she has improved her work, and this improved practice has influenced Mr J's confidence and consequently his capacity to contribute.

Mary can say that she has realised her values in her practice. She can make her claim to knowledge, and show that the claim has been generated through the rigorous procedure of producing validated evidence from systematically monitored practice.

Contrary to what some critiques have to say about whether it is possible to show links between one's own practice and the quality of educational experience of someone else, it would appear that showing these links is not only possible but essential in our claims to professionalism. Action research is a highly rigorous process which goes far beyond method and becomes a form of praxis.

Validation is an essential part of the process of making a claim to knowledge, and this is the focus of the next chapter.

8 Validating claims to knowledge

Validation is to do with people agreeing that what you say is believable. Research has an aim of advancing knowledge. You are claiming that because you have undertaken your research you now know more than you did. You are presenting your I-enquiry as a valid form of knowing.

This chapter deals with the questions:

- What is validated?
- Who validates?
- How do we validate?

What is validated?

Chapter 2 made the point that practice is rooted in personal knowing. Humans possess internalised (or individual, or implicit) knowledge, something we are not necessarily conscious of but which informs our practice nevertheless. We needn't have heard of Piaget, Habermas or Schön to be good practitioners. Rational thinking can even sometimes get in the way, as Kevin Costner in *Tin Cup* showed when he thought too much about his golf swing and lost his capacity to hit the ball straight.

Practice can be enhanced, however, when we reflect on what we are doing and decide to improve it. In action research this means becoming aware that we have

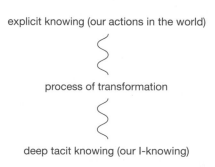

explicit knowing (our actions in the world)

process of transformation

deep tacit knowing (our I-knowing)

Figure 8.1 Transforming tacit into explicit knowledge

a vast fund of personal knowledge, valuing it, and understanding at a cognitive level how to use it for others' benefit. We raise our deep tacit knowledge which contains our values base to an explicit surface level where we try to live our values in our practice. We come to understand how our I-knowledge is embedded within and informs our practices in the world (see Figure 8.1).

For me, the most interesting and important part of this model is the process of transformation. What happens in the process of making tacit knowledge explicit? The struggle to make sense *is* the research – see Mellor's comment (p. 3).

The struggle to make sense is an ongoing process. We never get to a point of closure. Everything in life is full of its own potentialities for growth, unstable, in a process of transforming itself into a new, more fully realised form in the drive towards ongoing life. The whole of reality exists in a balanced state of tension, an inherent harmony of contradiction. Whatever is, is already changing. What appears as a new balanced state is already realising its own potential for change. This includes the process of knowing. Knowing involves a dialectical process of making tacit knowledge explicit, becoming aware of embodied knowledge and drawing theories out of practice, so that theory becomes embodied practice and embodied practice has the potential to emerge again as new theory. Here is the balanced tension where, as soon as we arrive at a point of saying, 'I know', we also know that we still have much to learn.

Often people working in traditional forms of scholarship find it difficult to accept this volatile process of knowing and coming to know as a legitimate process (see, for example, Newby, 1994). They cling to the idea that rational knowing is the only legitimate form; the only justifiable belief is belief in an objective reality. Subjectivity is suspect; the complexity and unpredictability of life are systematically factored out or ignored, as is the values base which informs human living. It is assumed that reality can be understood as a unified and predictable whole and that people and their practice should be adjusted to fit accordingly. Anyone who does not conform is regarded as anarchic.

Rational knowledge is validated using traditional forms of analysis (Schön, 1995). Traditional research has as major aims to show a cause-and-effect relationship between phenomena, and to judge outcomes in quantitative terms. Research which demonstrates causal relationships is regarded as good scientific research; research which is rooted in personal knowing is regarded as unscientific and lacking in rigour.

These rationalists have a point. While personal claims to knowledge can be justified and valid (if I say I have toothache I am making a valid claim to knowledge but it cannot be demonstrated to be true), these claims cannot stand alone in research contexts without some form of corroborating evidence. If a practitioner claims that they have improved their practice, they need to provide supporting evidence to show in what way the practice has improved and by what criteria they are making the claim. With these conditions, action research can be seen as a disciplined enquiry, where a practitioner systematically investigates how to improve practice and produce evidence for the critical scrutiny of others to show how the practice can be judged to have improved.

What is validated are the I-enquiries of people as they generate knowledge about their own work in company with others, and show the transformative process of coming to know. They explain what they hoped to achieve and how they feel they have achieved it by pointing to critical instances from the data which can be regarded as evidence. They explain how they are generating their own theories of practice from within the practice, and that the process of theorising is an ongoing dialectical engagement with inherently volatile problematics. Validating such personal practical theories involves moving beyond standardised categories of analysis, not an easy thing for many traditionalists, some of whom prefer not to engage and refuse to recognise the claim or indeed the need to develop new ways of thinking themselves.

Who validates?

Who do we choose to validate our work? Habermas (1979) says that the criteria needed to judge the legitimacy of knowledge claims are that

- a statement is true;
- the speech act is comprehensible;
- the speaker is authentic;
- the situation is appropriate for these things to be said.

Therefore, when we invite people to judge the validity of our claims to knowledge, we need to agree that:

- what I say about my practice is true;
- we use words and expressions that we all understand;
- we are sincere and avoid any deception;
- the situation is right for us to be discussing this issue.

It is, of course, less problematic to invite friendly critics rather than sceptical ones to comment on the work, but if we want our work to be judged in the wider community as worthwhile scientific enquiry, we need to ensure from the start that appropriate rigour is built in. Action research accounts need to stand on their own feet. Even though some people might disagree with the idea of action research (ontological perspectives), they should not have grounds to find fault with the methodological or epistemological rigour of the accounts.

It is perhaps wise to start with the most supportive critics and work outwards to the general public. One would therefore appeal to the following audiences.

Self-validation

As I continue my life work I have come to be my own stringent critic. I have learnt to interrogate the assumptions underlying my own thinking, and to check that I am speaking out of the values of respect for others and the need to see each point of view as worthy. While I disagree profoundly with some people's points of view and try to persuade them to think and act differently (for example, I do not think cruelty and wanton killing can ever be justified), I respect their right to hold their own opinion. I recognise my right also to hold my opinion, but I try to check that what I say honours others' right to do the same. This is how I interpret John Gray's (1995a) idea of agonistic pluralism. So I test my claims to knowledge against these values, and if I feel that I am living them out, I am prepared to defend my claims.

Colleagues' validation

At the same time I recognise that I am prone to self-delusion and factual error or misinterpretation, and I need to invite others to look at my work and give honest feedback about the claim to knowledge. These others include the following.

A critical friend

In any action enquiry it is as well to invite one or several critical friends to be involved throughout. They will become familiar with the research and will offer advice and criticism. Critical friends need to be supportive, but not so supportive that they do not point out real or potential flaws. Listen to their advice; sometimes one becomes too close to the action to see potential problematics, and fresh perspectives are to be welcomed.

A validation group

Aim to convene a validation group of several people for the duration of the research. Their commitment is to meet with you regularly, perhaps every six weeks or so, and offer feedback. You might want to convene the group at points of critical incidents, such as when you feel you are making real progress in terms of your identified success criteria and have powerful evidence to present.

A procedure for convening a validation group could be:

- Well before the meeting, enclose a report of the research so far, and say clearly what you are claiming to know.
- Ask the members to consider questions such as:

  ○ Is the report a valid description of an educational process?
  ○ Does the evidence support the claims that you are making?
  ○ Can they see instances where you are living out your stated values?

- Look carefully at the evidence at the meeting, discuss it, and invite approval for the claim to knowledge. Also invite suggestions how the research might be modified and strengthened.

Academic validation

If you are presenting a formal report you hope that the claim contained in the report will be recognised as adding to an existing body of knowledge. At the moment, the Academy is still the highest authority in what counts as legitimate knowledge (although the situation is changing in our post-industrial and knowledge-creating society), so the work has to stand in terms of its academic rigour. Herein lies a dilemma, however, because the criteria and standards of judgement used by the Academy tend still to be those of technical rationality, and a good deal of gate-keeping goes on to protect the status quo. This is one reason why action research accounts need to demonstrate internal methodological consistency, so that work cannot be rejected on technical grounds.

This brings us to the next point which is largely to do with power and politics.

How do we validate?

When you say you know something it is not only your brain or some part of it that knows. It is you, as a person. Knowing is more than cognitive activity, although it involves cognitive activity. It is whole-body practice. When we consider a person's claim to knowledge we do not study their brain; we consider what they do.

There are two sets of dilemmas in relation to how action research reports are judged. The first is to do with whether action research reports should be judged in terms of traditional research; the second is to do with the kinds of criteria set to judge them. Both sets of dilemmas are interlinked.

Reports are judged by criteria set by the audience who are scrutinising them. If the work is in a business context, for example, it will be judged in terms of a marketplace philosophy; if it is judged by a traditional academic audience it will be judged in terms of normative academic standards. In earlier times, when traditional technical rational approaches reigned supreme, action research was usually judged in terms of traditional conventions and criteria. Because traditional scholars tend to talk about research in abstract conceptual terms, rather than as a lived experience, research practice has usually been judged in terms of accepted theoretical concepts. There are many such concepts and conventions: for example, the ideas of replicability and generalisability, or the inclusion in a report of a literature review. Traditional scholars require that research complies with traditional conventions, otherwise doubt is cast on whether an account can be regarded as good quality research, or even research at all.

Debates have raged for decades, and the situation has now changed, though progress still needs to be made. Some new paradigm researchers, however, complain that their work is still judged in traditional terms; for example, the quality of reporting is still often considered more important than the quality of the practice recounted in the report. Thomas (1998) speaks of 'the tyranny of method', complaining that a focus on the technical issues of expertise in terminology and the inclusion of required ingredients such as a literature review lead to stereotypical reporting and foster stereotypical thinking about practice. He is not alone in his impatience with the idea that rationality is the only guarantee of truth; even Habermas in recent writing (1990) 'addresses the absence of the affective by stressing the requirement of solidarity in an ideal speech situation – a concern for the well-being of others and an empathetic disposition' (McDermott, 2000: 8).

Many paradigm battles have today been won; action research is now recognised as a legitimate research methodology in its own right. Issues such as replicability and generalisability are no longer seen as appropriate criteria for action research. This means that new criteria are being established about how action research reports should be judged; but this issue of how action research reports are judged has itself now become highly contested territory. The difficulty lies, as noted throughout this book, in whether action research is understood as an object to be studied and spoken about or as a practice to be lived and experienced.

The issue arises: if action research is an object to be studied and spoken about, then action research reports can be presented as only linguistic descriptions of activities; in this case, linguistically expressed criteria are sufficient for judging the report. If, however, action research is a practice to be lived and experienced, then action research reports can offer explanations for improving practice, in which case there is a need to go beyond only linguistically expressed criteria and communicate the action in different ways. For example, if the aim is to teach appreciation of music, how would one judge whether a student really appreciated a piece of music? A linguistically expressed criterion would be something of the kind 'Can show appreciation of music.' Such appreciation could be shown by asking the student to complete a questionnaire and tick an appropriate box, but there is some doubt whether this would really indicate appreciation of music. It might, however, be more appropriate to ask the student to produce a piece of music, or listen to one, and show how they felt that producing or responding to music was a valuable experience for them. To express this experience in a report, however, would require more than simple words; it would necessitate a demonstration of what the student felt and how their feeling affected their practice. The criteria would be living, demonstrable criteria, rather than mere linguistic ones.

Richard Winter's (1989: 43–65) work has been seminal in suggesting new kinds of criteria for assessing action research reports. He says that reports should demonstrate six principles.

- Offer a reflective critique in which the author shows that they have reflected on their work and generated new research questions.
- Offer a dialectical critique which subjects all 'given' phenomena to critique, recognising their inherent tendency to change.
- Be a collaborative resource in which people act and learn as participants.
- Accept risk as an inevitable aspect of creative practice.
- Demonstrate a plural structure which accommodates a multiplicity of viewpoints.
- Show the transformation and harmonious relationship between theory and practice.

These linguistic criteria, essential starting points, now need to take on flesh and bones. Action research reports need to show these criteria in terms of people's real living.

Jack Whitehead (2000: 99) believes that action research reports can be judged in terms of whether the author shows that they are offering explanations rather than only observations and descriptions of practice by living out their declared values:

> What makes the educational standards of reflective practitioners differ from traditional, 'linguistic' standards is that the living standards are embodied in the lives of practitioners and require ostensive definition to communicate their meanings. I am indebted to Moira Laidlaw [1996] for the insight that the meanings of the values I use as my educational standards [or criteria] are themselves living and developmental in the course of their emergence in practice.

Such living standards are a far cry from traditional categories of analysis which appear as linguistic checklists, such as those of the Teacher Training Agency (1998). They also require new forms of representation. In current work (Whitehead, forthcoming) Jack Whitehead is showing how multimedia presentations can display the reality of people's practice more adequately than verbal reports and can move the entire account into explanatory domains. Work undertaken by the National Centre for Technology in Education in Ireland has a similar focus, and colleagues are showing, through the media of ICT, how it is influencing the quality of learning in classrooms (McNiff, 2001). These are exciting times when the educational research community is shifting paradigms not only in terms of what counts as knowledge and how knowledge is generated, but also in terms of how claims to knowledge can be presented and how the influence of those claims can be disseminated in wider contexts.

In summary I would say that the process of validating claims to knowledge is moving beyond autocratic activities such as checking whether traditional elements of report writing are accurately executed, towards new dialogical forms of engaging with the report as an authentic representation of a life lived in an educational way. The validation process becomes educational for the validator as much as for the presenter. Validation is not the summative point in a programme that has led to closure, but a formative engagement in an experience which contains emergent property for the realisation of new potentialities.

I have now painted myself into a corner. I am making a case for ostensive explanation as a feature of action research reports, yet nowhere in this book do I include ostensive explanations – no pictures or videos, no forms of representation other than words to communicate the learning. You might believe me when I say that ostensive evidence of my learning exists elsewhere, but I have not included it here. Oh dear. Here's an agenda for new research: how can I include in future reports ostensive evidence of how I have encouraged others to learn and so contributed to a good social order? It would be so easy to do, now I think about it. In the next part of the book I have presented case studies by people whom I have supported in their studies, and they have produced ostensive evidence as part of their reports. I could have found ways also to include that evidence with this text – perhaps inclusion of a CD in the back cover flap, an inexpensive and convenient way of presenting visual evidence. Jack Whitehead has made a start with such presentations in the multimedia section of www.actionresearch.net. As I said, I have become critical, and that means evaluating whether one is living out one's own words, so at least here is evidence of the exercise of critique. I've said elsewhere that I like Iris Murdoch's (1985: 62) notion that when Jesus said, 'Be ye therefore perfect,' perhaps he could have meant, 'Be ye therefore slightly improved.' I am possibly slightly improved but clearly still have a long way to go.

Part III

How do we share our knowledge?

Stories from action researchers

This section contains case stories from four action researchers: Christopher Mc Cormack, Conchúr Ó Muimhneacháin, Ray O'Neill and Kevin McDermott. Several important issues emerge in the stories.

- Action research is an appropriate form of continuing learning in a variety of contexts.
- Action research can be seen as a form of problematic learning, not as a pathway to a specific outcome.
- Workplace dilemmas are often related in a deep way to forms of knowledge.
- The idea of action research needs to remain fluid and problematic.

All authors have studied with me on accredited courses. In presenting the stories I also want to show how I believe I have contributed to the authors' learning by encouraging them to be creative with ideas and critique their own practice. They were, of course, creative and critiqued their own practice before we began working together, but I like to think that my influence is in there somewhere, that I have encouraged them to intensify their awareness of their potentials for creating new ways of thinking and acting. If you feel that I am justified in saying this, then I would regard your opinion as validating my claim to knowledge, as spelt out in the Introduction. I would claim that my work is enabling me to contribute to the development of good social orders through education.

A comment that although all these stories are by men, stories by women appear in other parts of the text, and throughout my writings in general.

9　Action research in the home

Christopher Mc Cormack

This is an account of a small-scale piece of action research which I undertook as part of my studies for the Advanced Diploma at University College, Dublin, under the guidance of Jean McNiff, our tutor. Because I am retired from teaching, I worried that I would not be able to undertake an action research project into how I might improve my practice. Jean emphasised that action research was appropriate to studies which were located in informal as well as formal settings. I therefore present this account to show that I not only did the project but that the 'project' has become part of a new life work. I have learnt about how to improve my own situation, and I can also show how I have learnt, and continue to learn, much about myself, and my relationships with others. Although I have retired from formal work, my learning and work continue, though in significantly different ways from before.

My context

I came to Kells, County Meath, in 1963, and married Una Skelly in 1966. We now have a family of four who all live away from home but keep in regular contact. In September 1999 I retired from teaching at Kells Community School. Una had been a teacher of home economics at the same school, and she had retired two years previously.

Retirement (blest retirement, as Goldsmith would have it) poses its own problems: separation from colleagues and the world of work to which one's sense of identity and status in the community attach. For Una and myself the challenge was to forge a new world for ourselves.

We tend to speak of retiring *from* something, as if retirement has no reality and is a kind of deprivation. For Una and me it presented an opportunity to secure and enhance the quality of our lives together in a new situation. My belief was that the quality of life between us was indeed good, but that there was room for improvement. This is a social and moral question. How could the social space occupied by Una and myself expand to confer freedom, meaning and fulfilment for both of us by producing a mutually enriching dynamic?

This became the focus of my action research project. Although I was no longer teaching, I could come to view our lives together as my/our project, and to see the substantive learning involved in terms of how we both aimed to improve the quality of our lives together.

My project

Improving the quality of our lives was a wide and vague brief. In spite of Jean's advice to 'identify an aspect we want to improve' and 'keep it small, focused and manageable' (McNiff *et al.*, 1996: 52), what the narrow focus might be remained a mystery, at least for the time being. There is about undertaking an action enquiry that sense of unsettlement, when one has to let the practice speak for itself; only then, as Thomas à Becket says, is 'the meaning clear'. So for the moment I had to be content with the question 'How do I improve the quality of our life together?' so that values and practice concur, so that life becomes lived values.

Gathering, analysing, and reflecting on the data

As part of the research process I had to establish what the situation was. What was the quality of our life together? Una and I both decided to keep diaries. Initially we weren't too sure why we were doing this, but we submitted, even surrendered, to the experiment, and tried to let the events speak for themselves, while we resolved to reflect on them systematically.

To try to get an objective outsider's view I also asked my son John and my daughter Anne Marie to do an 'As it is' report. Anne Marie happened to have arrived from Letterkenny. She was staying overnight, so I asked her to do a quick snapshot of how things were. I asked John, who was also staying with us, to do the same. I also phoned a colleague in school, a longstanding friend of the family. I did this for various reasons, and in Una's presence:

- to try to clarify for myself what I was trying to do;
- to reassure Una that she was centrally involved;
- while clarifying for myself I was also clarifying for Una.

I asked the colleague to send me a report of her perception of the main issues arising in the conversation, but the report never materialised.

I began to analyse the data and identify issues. Excerpts from Anne Marie's letter establish that 'things never change'. She observes about me: 'The status quo – that's Daddy's motto: "Sure, isn't it grand the way it is"!' An analysis of John's report reveals that I am evidently 'highly functional, with a goal-oriented approach'; in my motoring I 'dislike unknown routes, lanes, lights, roundabouts'; my talk is 'functional but getting a bit better at small talk since retirement'. John's assessment also speaks about the need to be open to new ideas and protecting self-time as a way of achieving this.

31.1.00 I examine my diary. I examine John's write-up. I study Anne Marie's letter. Una and I exchange diaries. The purpose of the exercise is to establish the factors which impinge on improving the quality of life between Una and myself.

I am struck by some entries in Una's diary:

20.1.00 I am up at 9.30. Chris left towel stuffed behind radiator. Chris peels potatoes.

21.1.00 Computer. I'm not allowed to use it.

I began to reflect that clearly some things needed attention. To clarify the situation, I decided to ask Una if she would make a tape-recorded conversation with me about the quality of our life together. This would establish what needed improving and how I might set about doing this. John's and Anne Marie's 'As it is' accounts were helpful here. From their feedback I had become aware of my tendency to keep things as they were and my liking for concrete solutions to problems. Their observations tallied with some of my own diary entries:

20.1.00 9 a.m. I am up and around.
        11a.m. I took Anne Marie's car to the garage to have it serviced. My mood was one of frustration. I had been working on my lecture notes. I said to Una, 'I can't concentrate on anything.' Perhaps my studies are excessively invading my time for others? Almost every issue in action research, it seems to me, becomes a matter of time management and time protection. Every society is a relationship in which we contract to time-share: husband–wife, teacher–pupil, teacher–teacher. A willingness to time-share is a sense of values and a necessary dynamic to the society we engage in. Action research allows issues to be talked through and negotiated.

It began to emerge how I might begin to refine the focus of my project by concentrating on something to do with time management: others have claims on my use of time and I need to negotiate this, possibly by renegotiating agreed priorities.
    I noted further diary entries:

21.1.00 Computer e-mail. Una was frustrated with me. 'You never let me use it.' I made no comment but noted the remark. I felt it was significant. Perhaps we should have had a discussion on it there and then.

24.1.00 I record in my diary that I am getting a better grasp of the action research project. I am aware of constraints of time, of narrowing the focus, and of planning and reporting on a project.

25.1.00 I went to a funeral of my cousin in Roscommon. Una told me to take time with my relations. This reminded me of a comment made by John in his report: 'Dad should plan and talk things out and go out a bit more.'

26.1.00 I wrote out my action research notes. I said I'd vacuum the bedroom – wanting to help or dropping a hint?

28.1.00 Una went to see the film *Angela's Ashes* in Mullingar with her sister. I was delighted she was going, but glad that someone else had arranged it. Here is my problem with time again.

31.1.00 I studied 'As it is' reports.

2.2.00 At 10 p.m. I returned from UCD. Una, who has arthritis in her hands, had asked a neighbour if she knew of someone who would do some housework. I noted, but didn't comment just then.

4.2.00 This was my birthday. Cards, phone calls, Una's sister called.

5.2.00 I reflected on my diary entries and on John's and Anne Marie's assessments.

Emergent issues

Issues were becoming evident.

I asked Una if we could go ahead with the tape-recorded conversation. In preparation we agreed to list points emerging from our diaries. This conversation was a crucial point in my project. I anticipated that some issues would arise: that I dislike change, that I rarely plan to talk to so and so, that I should be more flexible and open minded, that I socialise more, and that I manage and protect family time. In my diary (3.2.00) I had written: 'Now probably the point is made that I could listen better and perhaps not have fixed ideas with my mind made up.' I was also aware of the issue of the computer and had recorded, 'I'm very possessive about the computer and Una said to me one day, "You won't let me use it." That's probably very true. And also that I could be a bit more supportive: ". . . things like curtains that were put up, you could praise them a bit more."'

The conversation indeed revealed that these issues were important.

We sat together and looked at our diaries.

Una   Just to recap: on what you have written about the fire. I left the fire and waited for you to get more coal, and eventually when I got up to get it you said you'd get it and the fire was nearly out at that point. I have the computer down and I put on it 'Show me how'. The towels in the bathroom: fold them instead of stuffing them behind the radiators: they just don't dry. The potatoes: you do peel them more or less every day. You do the hot-water bottle for me at night which is grand; you take the messages in and out of the car; you're very good with the lunch on Sunday, with setting the table and whatever has to be done. You helped me put up the curtains; you get the paper one or two days since we started doing the diary and it's a nice change – do it more often. You've already mentioned my hands. You put out the bin and empty the dishwasher quite a lot, carry the messages – little things, batteries and remote control for the television.

Chris It would appear from all that that I'm the ideal husband, that I've no need to do any action research! But I think there is. There are things we've spoken about before, like the computer. I do believe it's important. I think I need to change my attitude towards it. I'm trying to do that now.

As the conversation went on, however, it took on its own dynamic. Instead of addressing the burning issues, we agreed instead to go for a daily morning walk.

The transcript of the tape documents this change. The walk became the priority. I decided to stay with this new focus for the time being, but I wondered long and hard why we didn't get to the important issues.

Una and I decided on the following success criteria for our walk:

- the walk would take place every morning;
- we fixed the time for 10 a.m. (except on Sundays when we needed to be more flexible to allow us to prepare the Sunday lunch);
- we would walk hail, rain or snow, as Una put it;
- we would decide on wet gear and acquire it;
- the road selected was the Cavan Road, Kells;
- length of walk was initially to the De Royal factory.

From a methodological perspective, success criteria are important for a number of reasons:

- they establish a record of how one proposes to carry out a project;
- they are a standard by which the success of a project can be evaluated;
- they become a syllabus for action, because they help one to visualise in advance what is needed in order to achieve the aims of the project;
- they make the project public: they provide a kind of mission statement for the parties involved which imposes a discipline on the project. There is then a sense of shared responsibility for the success of the project.

Implementation

We are to start walking!

Now the entries in my diary focused largely, though not exclusively, on whether we met the criteria for success we had set ourselves.

6.2.00 We got a phone call from Anne Marie telling us that Shane and herself had got engaged. Great excitement all round. Una rang all the relations. Then we went for a walk.

Every day's entry after this records: 'went for a walk'.

Objectively, then, we were succeeding in carrying out the task we had set ourselves. But do the criteria tell us everything? Are they adequate? Is there a fuller dividend in the exercise for Una and myself? I began to wonder whether we had set ourselves an adequate description of what we wanted from the project. Should we have expected more of ourselves than the rather mechanical performance of a specified activity? I felt we needed to take stock.

Further data-gathering and reflection

I asked Anne Marie again when she and Shane were down home on Sunday if she would do an 'As it is *now*' account. Her account is honest, if not very dramatic.

'So! Has anything changed? It's difficult to say after such a short time. My idea of this project was for Daddy to improve some area of his daily living. It was for Mammy and Daddy to decide what those areas were . . . Did I want anything to change dramatically? Probably not . . . Home is home and it's familiar . . . Daddy and Mammy may see subtle changes between themselves and these may be for the better, but from my limited view, the folks are still the folks, and that's why I like them.'

However, I was beginning to perceive a few changes for the better. My diary entries began to take on a new perspective:

22.2.00 A walk is a good thing in itself. It has given me a new awareness of managing and protecting some family time. I had got perhaps too engrossed in my UCD studies and the walk at least protected that time space. It also provided an opportunity for just talking on whatever took our attention: conversation for its own sake. Walk time is talk time.

In a second taped conversation on 29.2.00 Una and I commented specifically on a new sense of enhanced physical well-being. Una remarked, 'There's no noticeable difference in my weight and that was one of the points of it, but I'm glad I'm doing it and hopefully will continue to do so.'

We also spoke about other issues:

Chris With regards to the computer now: we didn't set any criteria as to how we'd judge ourselves on that. If I were to ask you what you want out of the computer?
Una I just want to be able to use it.
Chris To use it. Right. That will involve a while together on it, but we don't need to schedule it.
Una No.
Chris Not at any particular time. Just when we're available. Anyway, Una, it's there. You know yourself. Just go ahead and practise on it.

Later in the conversation:

Chris What else do we need to look at?
Una I've asked a few people if they knew of anyone I could get to help with the house, who would come in for an hour or two. Nothing yet, but I'll keep looking.
Chris That's it then, and, Una, I'm very grateful for your helping me with this project. Thanks a million.

Reflection

What have I learnt? I have an enhanced sense of the interdependence of people in creating their own society. We live in the social space of others and we can expand that social space by allowing each other the maximum freedom. The dynamic which is created is the quality of life we speak of, which is not only spoken about but also practised. We learn to negotiate with others. (Jean exemplified this in her work with us at UCD, when she suggested we negotiate our syllabus, our assignments, and the criteria by which we wished our work to be assessed, something I had not previously experienced in my learning.) My experience of doing action research has shown me the need to work at a relationship and not just to assume it. I am reminded of Mr Collins's proposal of marriage to Elizabeth Bennett in Jane Austen's *Pride and Prejudice*. He says, 'I am convinced that it [marriage] will add greatly to my happiness.' Now in action research this statement can be made without irony, without selfishness, because of the mutuality of the relationship. It has to add to 'my happiness' or it will not add to Una's happiness and so benefit the relationship.

Undertaking action research is a social thing. It is about people caring for one another and about creating that social space in which this care is given concrete expression. I have reflected much on this, and related my experience to the literature I have taught during my professional life. I am thinking, for example, of Wordsworth's return to Tintern Abbey after a lapse of five years. In the pressure of the moment he evokes the past and then recreates it, realising that he still has much to do (What have I learnt? How can I improve?). The poet has matured and sees life reflectively.

And so . . .

And so back to the action. My project finished officially; I wrote up my report and received full marks; Una was always, and remains, my critical friend, so the honour is hers as much as mine. However, the project continues. Una and I continued to walk and talk, to reflect and negotiate the spaces of our lives. I improved in some areas. Una's diary of 3.3.00 records: 'Towels folded.' I had by now become very aware of my own need to continue learning and changing my ways and attitude. Consequently, for Una and me, retirement became an adventure to be undertaken, not an end point of a life already lived.

And as time has passed, we have begun to develop a deep appreciation of ourselves in relation with each other, to appreciate and anticipate the other's needs without words being spoken. I saw Una's frustration at not having the strength in her hands to vacuum, and one day I surprised myself as much as Una by taking the vacuum from her. While I hummed my way down the stairs and through the living room, Una went and quietly started working away at the computer.

10 Expect the unexpected

Conchúr Ó Muimhneacháin

This chapter recounts how I have discovered a deeper understanding of my educational values and beliefs through trying to live them in my work with colleagues, students and parents, as well as fellow researchers on the MA in Education course. Uncovering and clarifying these values through a process of reflection and dialogue have helped to make explicit the tacit knowledge which underpinned my practice. The research has also enabled me to rethink the relationship between curriculum, learning and teaching, and to reshape student learning tasks so that student achievement may be assessed in a way that is congruent with their learning experience.

My context is that I am joint co-ordinator of the Transition Year programme in a large all-boys school. The Transition Year option takes place between junior and senior cycles. It aims to offer students an opportunity to enjoy a one-year liberal and holistic educational experience, free from the external pressures of examinations; the goal is to encourage students to become autonomous, participative and responsive citizens (Government of Ireland, 1996). Great premium is placed in this programme on teachers' resourcefulness, creativity and willingness to develop new methodologies to realise the vision.

I wanted to develop a form of assessment that reflected the new educational priorities. I was, however, still stuck in a system that valued traditional forms of assessment, such as written tests. I came to realise over time how I was also, at the beginning of my research, pressured to conform to an outmoded way of thinking, and how I systematically and deliberately freed myself to live in ways which reflected the unpredictable and spontaneous nature of education and life itself.

When I began studying for my masters degree I encountered the ideas of educational research paradigms. Through my study I became aware of the significant influence positivism had had on framing my assumptions about what knowledge is and how it is acquired. I realised that I sought closure in my work. I also realised how the comfort of stability denied the dynamic reality which teaching presents. I had become a technician.

I wanted to live out my values of autonomy and justice. My rapidly changing thinking now resisted a view that my practice could be generalised, or that students as people could be manipulated, controlled and measured for the purpose of constructing and predicting yet another fixed solution. I began to extend these ideas about how learning might be assessed. I came to the idea of student presentation, a practice in which students would critique and account for their own learning, and also show their understanding of the processes through which they might claim that they were accountable. Student presentation as a form of self-assessment, however, was not a neat package that could be judged in traditional forms of scholarship such as its capacity for generalisability or replicability. Student self-assessment was a living phenomenon that needed to be judged in its own terms of how students were able to judge the quality of their own learning and its implications for their future lives. It was a process more than an end product.

I gained considerably from refocusing the ontological and epistemological lens through which I viewed the world. Through dialogue with my colleagues on the MA course and Jean McNiff, I began to question many of the assumptions which I had taken for granted until now: that research variables can be isolated, theory leads practice, research must be objective and value-free. This was a huge leap of faith for me, to put my personal theories of education on a par with those of philosophers, sociologists and psychologists. I reminded myself that there was much that I, and others who may wish to learn from me, could elicit from problematising issues that concerned me as I accepted the responsibility of interpreting the world from my own point of view (Polanyi, 1958).

Through my studies in action research, and through studying my practice, I see how I have been thrust into a spiral of continuous problematisation. Prior to the course I had vested authority in others which gave them control over my life. There was a certain stability and security in abstract systems of educational knowledge. But what was I gaining personally and professionally from the application of models and strategies? The realisation that answers to these questions left a lot to be desired prompted further examination. Self-discovery and reflection are not things that we have been very practised at in Ireland. Writing in a personal voice left me feeling exposed, yet helped me to realise that I had been noticeably absent in my own work. I have now gained confidence enough to demonstrate to others the relevance of such knowledge to my life and work.

The nature and scope of the enquiry

My research undertook to examine the systematic introduction and adoption of student presentation as a form of self-assessment. The research focused on how I was helping students to become aware of the central role they play in the learning process, and for them to recognise their own learning strengths.

I initially developed student presentation within my own class practice. The presentations took the form of three related phases. During a preliminary phase, students would demonstrate that they could set goals, that they could reflect and become self-aware, and also could plan and organise. This was followed by a presentation phase, which would demonstrate that students could present subject matters clearly, and could respond to peer observation and feedback. The third phase involved students' analysis of the feedback, and their construction of further goals.

I wanted to investigate the extent to which student presentation could act as a form of assessment which showed that students were developing as autonomous and self-aware individuals. I gathered data on these issues, and I supported students consistently at a personal level to see how they might improve their work. I tested the data and my provisional findings by inviting feedback from parents and students about whether the idea was leading to enhanced confidence and self-awareness. Feedback from parents and students was overwhelmingly positive. Buoyed up by the groundswell of support, and with my ideas now supported and reinforced, I set about trying to put a coherent framework in place which would establish student presentation as part of institutional assessment practices.

My initial intention was to introduce student presentation as a Transition Year initiative which would be supported by all staff. I outlined my ideas at a meeting of the Transition Year teachers in October 1999. I gave a description of the initiative and how I hoped it might develop. A vote was taken to decide whether to go ahead with the idea and, to my surprise, a sizeable minority of teachers were not in favour. I was devastated. However, to respect the opinions of that minority, my fellow co-ordinator and I decided not to proceed with the initiative until further clarification could be sought from all involved.

This rejection by others of an initiative in which I had invested so much of myself was not easy to accept. I perceived the struggle as one of radical and conservative perspectives. Perceptions of fairness seemed to be at issue. My belief that students should develop their own values, free as much as possible to make their own decisions and choose their words and actions (Strike and Soltis, 1985), seemed to be at odds with the belief system of others in the group of Transition Year teachers. I came to see that I had moved beyond the culture of positivism that still claimed them. I wondered whether they might one day come to see the limitations of such a culture.

I reflected on the situation, and used my journal at length to try to work out my own dilemmas. It dawned on me that student presentation did to a certain extent reflect the nature of the teaching that students experienced, and my colleagues must also have felt this. While I felt that my efforts to encourage student autonomy and the freedom to express their own ideas might be, in my eyes, good news, it might be perceived as a threat by others. I also began to see that action research is a methodology which does not aim to resolve a problematic external situation so much as a methodology by which one begins to work out dilemmas, including the dilemmas generated when a project goes in unanticipated directions, and how necessary it is to stick with the problematic and work it through.

I resolved to live by the courage of my convictions and develop student presentation on a smaller scale. I might not successfully influence institutional practice at a macro level, but I was reassured by critical colleagues who scrutinised my work that I was having some influence on my students' educational experience at a micro level. Implementation is indeed a tricky business (Fullan, 1992).

Consequently the focus of my research changed to an investigation of how I might develop student presentation as a form of assessment in a particular subject area. I reasoned that if I could produce concrete evidence to show that my ideas could be justified in terms of how student self-evaluation can lead to improved student achievement, I could bring that evidence to the staff at a later date to show that they might wish to try it out as a now validated methodology. My research therefore focused on how I could develop student self-assessment practices at the local level of my own teaching to encourage student autonomy. Because of the reaction of some of my colleagues, I decided not to extend the ideas of student presentation into other subject areas at this stage.

I began to see that the rejection of the initiative by colleagues was not an end to my project but itself a new departure. Through developing a deeper understanding of the work I was doing I felt that I had a legitimate right to challenge the status quo. In previous work (Ó Muimhneacháin, 1999) I had claimed that in the implementation of curriculum change, extension may be a more reasonable goal than conversion. I was investigating change, and I was also changing. I was realising that educative relationships demonstrate such dialectical interactions. I had come to see that in a situation of developing one's understanding of practice, the formation of supportive partnerships is highly significant to personal and professional growth.

Hogan (2000: 17) expresses well my experience of moving away from traditional forms of assessment:

> originality is often sidelined, or rendered colourless, by more insidious means than through the overt control of the management of schooling. Most significantly such emaciation occurs through assessment regimes which systematically reward a conformist kind of learning and which promote within the culture of teaching the unimaginative drill by which such learning is brought about.

I began to see, like Dewey (1916), that my quest for knowledge was an adventure which involved risk. I developed the confidence not to feel threatened by innovation and change, but to search out the unknown as a context which would lead to greater personal insights and a heightened sense of achievement and professional accountability.

The group project

I developed a new context for the research. As part of the Irish programme in Transition Year I introduced a group project on the theme of the Irish musical tradition. I wanted to encourage interaction among the students to promote interpersonal development. Individuals were at liberty to negotiate responsibility for sections of the project according to their individual strengths, thus valuing individual intelligence profiles through collaborative group work (Pollard, 1997).

The students and I also negotiated the assessment of the task. They chose to be assessed on the presentation of the group project rather than answer a question on the project as part of the traditional Christmas tests. I was pleased to accept their decision; the content of the project itself is less important than the social engagement such a project initiates, and how such negotiations have impact on future social lives.

The boys' decision created a moment of truth for me, however, in that I would now for the first time in my teaching career not have a formal written Irish test for Transition Year at Christmas. I related to Sockett's view of the need for courage: 'It is difficult to be courageous in times of accountability, performance evaluation, management by objectives, outcome based learning, and all the other bric-a-brac of the kind of institutional system we have developed, let alone its politics' (Sockett, 1993: 76). I was deeply concerned about the expectations of parents and fellow teachers. I became aware of my own fear of being exposed, of standing alone.

My principal was supportive when I talked through with him how I hoped to use student presentation rather than a written test as a form of assessment. His support strengthened my resolve.

Students' presentations

The students presented their individual reviews and group projects over two sessions. This was the moment of accountability for my students and a moment of integration for me, when I hoped everything would come together. In a wonderful atmosphere of buzz and excitement and tension, the boys spoke openly and honestly. They offered an outline of their involvement in the programme so far, and what that involvement had meant in terms of their educational experience. Some of their accounts were critical yet presented in a manner that was thoughtful and designed to be constructive. One student said: 'I have to say that I have been mildly disappointed by Transition Year and would say that it hasn't quite lived up to my expectations. This isn't to say that I haven't enjoyed the past few months, because I have, but I feel that Transition Year hasn't met its potential.' I recognised this statement as diplomacy at its best. I also recognised that this student was beginning to demonstrate what I and policy documents maintain are the principal benefits of Transition Year, though he was not yet articulating them: the capacity to form an opinion, to become self-aware, to take responsibility for one's own ideas and actions. I also recognised that I had succeeded in what I had set out to do: I had encouraged in students the confidence to speak in public and to critique with compassion.

To test my claim that I had succeeded in doing this, I asked two colleagues to say whether they felt I had developed my practice in a way that would encourage students to speak in public and critique with compassion. They had viewed the students' presentations, as well as observed my own lessons from time to time, and their comments included: 'You always acted with integrity towards the students. You established a culture of trust and care so that students felt they could speak without fear of recrimination.' 'You are justified in saying that you worked actively to encourage students to question. You encouraged them consistently to question you and their fellow students, and also in a way that showed respect and care for other people.'

Implications

The work has had significant implications for me, personally and professionally. I have come to see how collaborating with my students has moved me to respect their opinion and to promote a learning environment and negotiate a learning agenda which is not fixed in stone but is capable of being responsive and democratic. I have moved to a position where I wish to integrate all learning experiences in a meaningful way; I have learnt that curriculum is an integration of teaching and learning by students and teachers. While I do not underestimate the problems, I am excited about the possibilities within student presentation as an authentic form of assessment.

I became increasingly aware of the dialogical and unpredictable nature of learning, both the students' and my own. I came to see how I had to adapt my practice according to the wider social and political situation. In action research processes ideal situations seem rare. My research helped me to understand that change and integrating theory and practice involve complex and contradictory processes. I could also now compare my new thinking with the old. Traditional ways of doing research offered me a finished picture to stand back and admire. The picture I am creating in my present action research practice is a developmental and vibrant one. Each stroke changes the picture in an evolving depiction of my life story. It is a living, changing and gloriously messy masterpiece in the making.

I have come to relate strongly to Augusto Boal's view of theatre, and I see his ideas as informing my own on the nature of teaching for learning: 'Theater [and teaching] is change and not a simple presentation of what exists: it is becoming and not being' (Boal, 1992: 28). My research experience has given me the confidence and reassurance to continue my life work as a process of becoming.

11 Where will we put the computer?

Ray O'Neill

This sounds like a question that is asked in many homes when a new computer is bought for the family. Should it be kept in the sitting room or in one of the children's bedrooms? Problems of space and accessibility are very familiar at home but they seldom arise in school. Or do they?

In November 1997 the Taoiseach and the Minister for Education and Science launched *Schools IT2000*. This is an initiative intended to improve computer literacy in Irish schools. At the launch the Minister for Education told us: 'Helping teachers to develop the skills necessary to use information technologies has been shown throughout the world as being the key to successfully introducing them in the classroom' (Martin, 1997).

In response to this our school undertook a number of steps to enhance computer provision for students. As part of our resources, we obtained a computer that could be made available for school staff. The school management accepted that this computer would be for the use of teachers. Then the question arose: 'Where will we put the computer?' Management decided that the computer should be placed in the library. As a teacher I was not certain that this was the right place for it; I felt that the staff room was a better location.

My reasons for wanting to locate the computer in the staff room included the following: there is no librarian and the library is normally locked; to get into the library you have to go to the school office; when the secretary is free she gets the key from her desk which opens the key cabinet on the wall; inside the key cabinet is another locked cabinet; the key to the library is in here; you can then open the door of the library, start up the computer and get to work. If I were not very committed to the use of computers would I go to all that trouble? I think not. I can imagine management thinking: If they really want to use the computer they will go out of their way to use it.

I believe that instead of making it difficult for teachers to use computers we should be making it difficult for them not to use them. Those who favoured the staff room as a location for the computer won the argument, eventually. Subsequent changes in the use of the computer seemed to be quite significant. Before the computer went into the staff room, eight members of staff used a computer in school from time to time. Now, eighteen months later, only two members of our large staff do not use the school computer in some way. Those who use it have come to their present positions from different perspectives. Some could not wait for it to arrive. Others who initially had no interest began to see advantages. Some saw that by producing overheads on the computer they could save themselves a lot of work drawing diagrams on the blackboard. One teacher's son went backpacking in South America, and he took up emailing his son as a means of maintaining contact. This teacher is now developing geography content for the school intranet. Another teacher, who seemed to be determinedly anti-technology, while observing one of his colleagues was heard to say, 'If that eejit can use it so can I.' Two teachers regularly sit at the computer, one busily showing the other how to send emails, how to write notices, how to make overheads. Different teachers have come to use the computer by different routes, but almost all have started using it.

What is important is that teachers were given the opportunity to develop a relationship with the computer on their own terms. There was no pressure about when they should get involved or what they should do with the computer or even how. In many cases the initial use was not particularly serious. It involved things like emailing friends or finding out if Brazil won the World Cup in 1962. Teachers quickly moved on to producing notices, writing class notes, developing classroom materials.

The question 'Where will we put the computer?' raises issues greater than a question of location. These are about how we view education. People who saw the library as the appropriate location were, I believe, reflecting a view that knowledge has to be locked away and protected. The model involved is the one Schein (1996) in his three-cultures model calls 'The Engineering Culture'. People working in this culture hold values such as a preference for people-free solutions, an absolutist view of reality, that practices should be safety-oriented. Those who viewed the staff room as the best location were focusing on access and usability. They held a view that knowledge, education and learning should be available to all and on their own terms. In this view, education is participatory, emancipatory and controlled by the person being educated. An important element of this is the recognition of the autonomy of the learner (Habermas, 1973) and a willingness to empower the learner (Lomax, 1994).

The Minister was right. Helping teachers to develop the skills necessary to use information technologies is a key to integrating them successfully into the class-room. 'Where will we put the computer?' is a core question in helping teachers to gain the skills and confidence necessary for teaching ICT, and to ensure its positive influence for student learning. However, 'Where will we put the computer?' is not just a question of location. It is a question about how we view education. Is knowledge a rare commodity that must be protected and kept away from harm? Or is knowledge such a valuable commodity that it must be made accessible to all who want it even when they do not know they want it?

I am now the co-ordinator of the Schools Integration Project, an initiative developed by the National Centre for Technology in Education as the body responsible for the implementation of *Schools IT2000*. Colleagues and I have developed a school intranet, and as part of my work I am pursuing my doctoral studies to see how it might be possible to show the link between teachers' classroom pedagogies using ICT and the quality of student learning (O'Neill, 2000, 2001). I have encouraged school personnel to use and develop their confidence in ICT, and I have taken on the work of supporting teachers in this way.

These are exciting times to be a teacher of ICT in Irish schools. We are breaking new ground in our understanding both of technologies and how their use can encourage students to create and disseminate their knowledge. We are exploring means by which the knowledge can be shared using multimedia technologies, and we recognise that we are in new territories of knowledge dissemination. 'Where will we put the computer?' is a question that is at the heart of our educational epistemologies of practice. Where we put the computer reflects our commitments to education and learning.

12 My involvement in action research

Kevin McDermott

My introduction to action research was by accident. My colleague, the principal in the school where I teach, had been invited to an information session in the Marino Institute of Education in Dublin, on an initiative aimed at supporting teachers in developing their practice. He couldn't attend and asked me to go instead.

I had never heard of action research and was taken with the introduction given by Jean McNiff and Úna Collins, the then head of the Postprimary Department, who were developing the initiative (see McNiff and Collins, 1994), though I was suspicious of the enthusiasm with which they described the good life that could come into being through action research.

What arose from that meeting was the Marino Institute of Education Schools Based Action Research Project. In hindsight this was an extraordinary project. In exchange for saying, 'Yes, I'd welcome the chance to think about some area of my life in school,' I was invited to join in conversation with Jean and Úna and the other participants. Seven years later, that conversation continues, in particular with Jean, with Marian Fitzmaurice and Alec MacAlister, two teachers who took part in the original project, and with many other colleagues over the intervening years.

I still retain an attitude of scepticism towards action research (and all or any research paradigms) as a set of principles and procedures and a way of thinking, which will solve problems, or improve practice. I have been involved in reflecting on practice for a long time, without feeling the need to give my allegiance to any one form of action research or to action research itself. I have, quite happily, lived on the borders of different kinds of critical/reflective territories. Of course, the invitation to work in a reflective and reflexive manner has been immensely stimulating.

Perhaps the most rewarding insight for me has been the realisation that conversation is the site of the most searching reflection and the source of the most valuable insights. When Jean and Úna first visited me in school to talk about the work I was doing, I was struck by the conversational quality of our meeting and the attentiveness of their listening. We were not solely engaged in dialogue, in a form of logical exchange, but in something more exciting and affirming. The talk, the conversation, was other-seeking and open to going wherever it took us. The provisional, tentative nature of the work I was doing with the senior students in the school was explored in a way that did not rush me towards any certain conclusions. Indeed, the nature and quality of the reflection, enacted and encouraged through the conversation, was as much the focus of the discussion as the 'content' of the project.

Since then the focus of my work has been dialogue and conversation in a number of educational settings. In particular I have sought to develop my understanding and my practice of pedagogical conversation, a collaborative form of educative communication. I cannot honestly say that seven years on, I am seven times wiser and more knowledgeable on the subject. Insights, hard earned, are lost and forgotten and have to be re-achieved in the daily round of meeting and talking that constitutes education. But I continue to be in conversation with my colleagues, with myself, with various writers and researchers. And I revisit the reports I have written on my practice so that, to borrow a phrase from Barthes, my past is renewed upon contact with my present intelligence. And the texts which capture past practice are then open to the persuasive and creative power of redescription.

My contact with action research has given me confidence to place myself at the centre of my concerns and scepticism towards attitudes which would erase the 'I' from my enquiries. An attitude to enquiry that is reflective, reflexive and sceptical puts many taken-for-granted assumptions about research under pressure and results, in my experience, in a form of research that is creative and directed towards human flourishing. In my own work I have sought to make a critical self-insertion into the metalanguage of school, with a view to restoring the relationship between subject and object, heart and mind, which is often severed in the professional and academic discourse on school. My work is informed by the belief that teaching is, primarily, a relationship, and the existential bond between teacher and student is an affective one. I also believe that conversation is the form of communication best suited to expressing the pedagogic relationship.

Now, as I work to complete my PhD, I still feel the excitement of the adventure that seeks insights into my own practice as an educationalist and a researcher and that looks for better ways of seeing and better ways of presenting my insights. The work I have been engaged in has been searching and demanding from both an intellectual and an affective point of view. It has also been creating and self-forming.

By placing the self at the centre of the research, there is a sense in which there is no terminable point for the work of enquiry. In this regard I draw strength from the example of Socrates and others, including Freud and Lacan, who associated the potential of teaching with its willingness to acknowledge what is not known. The teacher is, interminably, a learner, engaged in an unceasing conversation with his/her self, within the context of social relations, and the institutions of schools and education.

Seven years on I'm thankful that the principal of my school couldn't attend the meeting that introduced me to the ideas of action research. And I look forward to the ongoing conversation.

Part IV

Contributing to good social orders through education

The focus of my research is how I might contribute to the development of good social orders through education. I am claiming throughout this text that I am achieving this, and I have produced what I consider to be valid evidence in support of the claim. I like to think that the stories in this book show how I have influenced people's learning and their capacity to make informed choices about their practice. However, I am aware that I need to spell out my understanding of the nature of a good social order so that my claim may be critiqued in its own terms; and also to make explicit what I feel is the nature of my contribution.

Chapter 13 explains my understanding of the nature and formation of good social orders. I make the point consistently that a good order is not something external to its members, but is embodied in the process of working in a way that may be demonstrated as good, in the sense that the process is evolutionary, beneficial and life-affirming for all.

Chapter 14 develops the point. If systematic enquiry is part of human striving to know more, and how to use that knowledge for social benefit, it follows that the process of enquiry itself must demonstrate the nature of a good order. Action research can be demonstrated to have the potential to influence the quality of learning experience for all. How this may be accomplished is shown here through the case-study evidence of Caitríona Mc Donagh. Her story is intimately linked with and enfolded within my own. Using her story as an exemplar, I try to show how I have supported others to have confidence in their claims to have contributed to the good by showing how their enquiries have fostered educative relationships and raised educational achievement. I try to show how I have influenced people's understanding without in any way diminishing the power of their own self-study of their learning and practice.

13 Action research and good social orders

I said in the Introduction that it is not enough to ask questions about knowledge production and dissemination without placing those questions within broader questions to do with human purposes. The questions 'What do we know?', 'How do we come to know?' and 'How do we share our knowledge?' need to be contextualised within questions which ask, 'Knowledge for what?' And it is important to remember that 'what' does not necessarily imply human benefit. If we believe that education is about encouraging people to see that they have choices about how they recreate themselves, we have to accept that they will often use their choices in ways with which we do not necessarily agree. In this view the 'what' could be to do with distribution of instruments of torture as much as with distribution of human aid. The 'what' in 'knowledge for what?' is the heart of the matter.

As noted earlier, putting the prefix 'educational' before 'action research' is considered by some a sufficient strategy to ensure that the idea of action research will refer only to humanitarian practices. This is no safeguard, nor should it be. One person's idea of education is no more and no less legitimate than another's; Hitler's is as valid as Dewey's. Whether we agree with what they have to say is not at issue. What is at issue is who decides the legitimacy of their opinion and how this is done.

Mandating on issues about legitimation raises problematics about whose criteria and parameters are valid. There are no universal guidelines here. Pragmatists would say that what works is its own legitimation; relativists would say that each culture has its own norms and standards by which legitimacy is legitimated. There is, however, no single overarching structure of values by which to judge such things. If we are all different, and claim the right to be different, we all have a right to be who we are within our own terms of reference. This is the point made by Berlin and others who believe in agonistic pluralism, and it is a key premise of this book. People are different and social lives are prone to conflict. Who can claim absolute knowledge about what counts as 'the good', and on what grounds?

My own position, as I have stated earlier, is to have come to abandon ideas about 'the good' as a situation to be aimed for. People simply disagree about things, and no one person can legislate. I doubt it is ever possible to come to a consensus about what counts as 'the good' in a substantive sense, and I would be worried if that were the case, for critique then disappears. I have abandoned the idea that 'the good' can be understood only as an abstract concept. Instead, I have come to see the idea of 'the good' always as related to people's lives. In coming to understand my own practice, and accepting that it is never fixed – my very ideas shift from one moment to the next as I think and rethink – I have come especially to see how processes of enquiry might themselves be construed as good orders. When people work with ideas, what is important, in my view, is the process of engagement, whether they treat ideas and the people who hold those ideas with respect or disdain; whether they see the ideas as holding merit or reject the ideas and their creators and close out critique. These views have informed my own practices of working with people who often hold conflicting opinions, and also led me to recognise that their ideas are frequently in conflict with my own.

I have come to see a dialectical relationship between the ideas of research and conflict. For me, these are not only abstract terms. They are human processes. As people try to find out and create new knowledge, what they present as true for them is inevitably contested by others who hold different beliefs. The process of research is always potentially conflictual (people disagree about what they come to know), and conflict is the site for new research (people try to find out how they can generate further knowledge, find ways of validating their claims, persuade others of their truth, and so work towards resolving the conflict). The process of research can be destructive, when one person closes down the opportunities of others for learning and negotiation, or life-affirming, when all parties recognise the potential value of one another's contribution.

I have come to understand that people live with conflict and work out their differences through conflict. Conflict in this view is not pathological; it is inevitable, and the site for negotiated settlements. For me, 'the good' is to do with processes which are life-affirming for all. Working through the conflict calls us to exercise our best efforts at tolerance, to suspend our prejudices and really try to understand the other. It requires us to see the other as a person, a 'thou' rather than an 'it' (Buber, 1937). By trying to understand and relate we realise our own potentialities for relation. The good order is not something we aim to create in the future; it is where we are now as we try to live in ways which are mutually respectful. 'The good' does not belong to any one person, though each person has to have a vision of what constitutes it. 'The good' is a collective process, in which life-affirming practices are enacted reciprocally. We create the future as we live the present. The good society is here, as we make it.

In terms of this book, I believe this is the heart of the matter – knowledge for what? – as the point on which action research stands or falls. If it is possible to make a case for what counts as a good social order (in terms of the discussion above, how the process of enquiry might be construed as such) and if it is possible to show how a person-centred dialectical process of enquiry can generate such a good social order, then the legitimacy of action research as a form of enquiry which leads to 'the good' can be established.

The relationship between individual knowing and collective knowing

Interesting movements are taking place in the literatures of the social sciences and education research in terms of the focus, or object, of enquiry (what is studied) and the methods of enquiry (how it is studied). Until quite recently there was a seemingly unquestionable assumption that the object of enquiry was a concept. Educational research aimed to understand 'education'; management and organisation studies focused on 'management' and 'organisation'. These concepts were seen as representing everyone's experience of education, management or organisation. The concepts became the things that researchers studied. The concepts had a life of their own; they were 'out there', separated from the researchers who were studying them.

Of course, this perception does not mirror reality. Reality is that education, management and organisation are about the real-life experiences of real people. In a commonsense view it is impossible to investigate concepts such as education, management and organisation without taking real experiences into account. However, the situation remained throughout much of human enquiry that it was sufficient and acceptable to study and analyse the concept without any recognition of real people. This has given rise to what is often called 'the theory–practice gap', the traditional separation of theory (how a concept is understood) and practice (what people do as educators, managers and practitioners).

The situation is changing in a good deal of contemporary work. In the foreword to their seminal text on new paradigm research, Rowan and Reason (1981) describe the shift away from traditional texts 'which spend a page or two on theory, ending with a statement that the experimental method is what it is all about really' (p. xi) to those which see 'the nature of the inquiry process itself as a particular form of human endeavour' (p. xii). In education studies the shift has been happening for a long time, and is demonstrated in comments such as this one from Usher (1996: 36, 49): 'Nowadays there is a general scepticism about the very possibility of value neutrality and a "disinterested" science . . . In educational research the need to problematise the practice of research is . . . now fairly common practice, particularly in the emphasis on action research and practitioner-based enquiry'. Pettinger's (1999: 1) text is an example of how the shift is happening in organisation studies, 'All organizations are communities of human beings . . . Human communities must be founded on common belief, and must symbolize the cohesion in common principles and mutuality of interest'. And Golding and Currie (2000: 1) emphasise that management should not be perceived as a unified set of techniques but rather as a problematic practice; and this view, radically 'contra' to traditional views, needs new methodologies to research it: 'a cyclical approach towards understanding the nature of management may be more appropriate than any approach that attempts to produce definitive statements about management'.

The shifts in these literatures are representative of a new focus on the individual throughout human enquiry. This point was made in Chapter 1, when I discussed how, in the second cognitive revolution which began in the 1950s, the focus of enquiry moved away from study of the behaviours of people by external researchers to trying to understand the reasons and intentions of those behaviours. Making public these reasons and intentions and efforts at understanding became the responsibility of people themselves who were making their own choices about how they lived their lives.

However, the new focus on the individual brings with it its own dilemmas, particularly in discussions about how individuals are located within groups of other individuals, the kinds of relationship they forge, and what the relationships are for. The dilemmas are particularly deep when the issue is one of knowledge. When an individual claims that they know something, how does that claim come to be accepted and legitimated by others?

When Margaret Thatcher said, 'There is no such thing as society,' she was in one sense right; in another, profoundly mistaken. Groups, or societies, wherever they are found, are always made up of individuals, so in one sense there are only collections of individuals. How individuals think and behave when they are on their own, however, is often quite different from how they think and behave when they are in company. The way that people organise themselves and develop their patterns of interaction and the principles which guide choices about which patterns to develop come to constitute social, cultural and political norms. If people fail to maintain a critical watchful eye on the norms they have agreed, the norms can become reified as systems, and, as Habermas (1973, 1979) has explained, the 'system' can take on a life of its own and move beyond the consciousness of the people who created it in the first place. Consequently, people come to serve the needs of the system, rather than the system serving the needs of the people. An example of this happened recently. Two years ago I had negotiated to develop a particular professional learning course with a university. University personnel agreed with my suggestion that the learning support provision would be one three-hour group meeting per month, and one hour's tutorial support per course member per month. From our experience of managing such courses, we felt this was an appropriate level of learning support. Now, two years after the course began, my own circumstances have changed, and I wanted to discuss with course participants how we might renegotiate times. My overtures were met with resistance by some who expressed concern that their learning support provision was being reconfigured. I found myself held hostage to an idea which I had proposed and developed but which had now become a reified system in its own right, beyond me and other users.

This issue is central: how the relationships between individuals and groups might be perceived as the performance context within which are embedded the relationships between individual knowing and collective knowing. How is it possible for an individual's I-system of knowledge to be recognised and legitimated? It is possible only if people are willing to recognise that other people think in ways different from themselves, and are prepared to be tolerant of individual differences. If some people operate from within one system of knowledge (an E-system, say), they might find it hard to accept an I-system of knowledge, in the same way that some teachers do not understand that students might think in ways differently from the ways they the teachers do (see Chapter 14). When we are caught up in established ways of knowing it is hard to move out of those ways and see that other ways exist that are more suited to others' needs. Often we do not even see that there is another way. We get trapped by our own stereotypes. Sometimes managers cannot perceive themselves as workers, and academics cannot see themselves as teachers. Getting stuck in bounded ways of knowing, getting stuck in the very idea that there is only one way of knowing and the way one already operates is right, is to shut down one's own potentiality for new learning; not, in my philosophy, a good thing.

Knowledge of and for the good

Knowledge is neither good nor bad. However, when it manifests as social practice it becomes value laden, for it is in social practice that issues of what counts as good or bad arise. How knowledge is used decides whether it should be designated 'of the good' or 'for the good'. This raises questions of how we understand 'good'.

I recently drove to Omagh from Dublin along the N2, a journey I have not undertaken for some time. At the border is the town of Aughnacloy, where a military checkpoint was located. All my previous experience of driving through the checkpoint has been one of eerie silence, a place holding its breath, 'No photography allowed', unseen watchers as you weave through the dark green corrugated iron and concrete. Amazingly, the checkpoint has disappeared. The land is sweet, grass smoothed out, no sign of occupation or shooting or fear. People come and go openly, and my journey from south to north and back again is as uneventful as the settling of snow on snow.

What has happened here to bring this place from silence to sound? Whatever has happened, and however it has happened, it has been of the good and for the good. The ideas of freedom and pluralism have become real in the lives of people; communities have chosen to live with conflict, not as a pathology, but as a site in which they have reached understanding through the struggle and can all go about their daily business on that basis.

We know what has happened – a peace process which has lurched forward amid torrents of blame and recriminations, amid the subversive and violent actions of last-stand die-harders who continue to make their point and strive for dominance. We know that somehow voices of compassion have remained consistent: we cannot agree on everything, we do not want to agree on everything, but we can agree to get on with our differences and stay alive. We can agree to keep talking, knowing that through our talk we will get to know one another better and see ourselves as persons in relation with other persons.

Peace is a process to be worked through, not a position to be arrived at. It is the same methodological principle as with action research. We find understanding by engaging with the problematics; we find forgiveness by developing the capacity to be compassionate and working through the hate; and we find hope in the capacity for self-renewal by embracing despair. These things are not at a distance from us. They are within us, part of a reality of which we also are a part and which we create from choice.

Libraries of books exist which try to define 'the good'. For me, it is within the relationships that people create together as they try to do the best they can to make life good for one another, a process always located within the intentionality of the individual, and always negotiated and enacted reciprocally with others.

Education for good societies

In this sense Dewey wins. Dewey's idea of education is that it is a process which leads to further education, a life-affirming process for all. Individual people are recognised as autonomous agents capable of infinite self-transformation who are working together as collectives of similarly capable autonomous agents, not out of a wish for consensus (which is frequently a source of unfreedom) but out of a sense of responsible committed action to create the kind of society in which they would wish to live. This vision is said well by Chomsky (1996: 75), who shares, with Dewey and Russell, a vision of what Russell called 'the humanstic conception': quoting Dewey,

> the belief that the 'ultimate aim' of production is not production of goods, but 'of free human beings associated with one another on terms of equality'. The goal of education, as Russell put it, is 'to give a sense of the value of things other than domination', to help create 'wise citizens of a free community' in which both liberty and 'individual creativeness' will flourish, and working people will be the masters [*sic*] of their fate, not tools of production.

In my view the methodologies by which we find the means to realise the vision are methodologies of responsible best guess, doing the best we can with what we have. The struggle is not to find the best way; the struggle *is* the best way, provided we recognise one another as part of the same struggle, similarly engaged in doing the best we can.

Knowledge for what?

The what, the heart of the matter, becomes how to create social orders in which the values of freedom and agonistic pluralism can become reality. In education research it is not how to demonstrate that one set of conditions leads to specific outcomes; it is how to show one's educative influence such that one child's quality of learning was improved. In professional education it is not to perform according to a checklist of competencies; it is how to demonstrate through the production of validated evidence that one accepts the responsibility of professional excellence as a form of accountability. In our approach to understanding what we are doing, it is not the production of linguistic reports about what should be done but the production of living reports to show what has been done and its potential to transform into new forms of good practice.

While the disciplines of human enquiry generate their specific bodies of factual knowledge, the ideas of knowledge production and its dissemination remain in the domain of education, the broad encompassing arena within which the disciplines are located.

In the view expressed in this chapter educational enquiry is not a procedure which leads to eventual understanding; it is a process of understanding itself, a speculative, adventurous process of creating ideas, testing them out to see if they might work, modifying them, and creating new ideas out of present ones. Theory is not the product of a process of critical discernment but itself a process of critical discernment. This view is in keeping with Schön's (1995) idea of the new scholarship, an approach to human enquiry which has its being within practice. Scholarship, says Schön, needs to move beyond the traditional categories of hard scientific analysis and technique, 'rigorously controlled experimentation, statistical analysis of observed correlation of variables, or disinterested speculation' (p. 29). It needs to develop new approaches, new principles to show the relational nature of practice and the lines of influence between people as they work out their lives together. This, he says, is action research, and, as demonstrated within this book, action research can happen anywhere, though it is not, and should not, always be called action research.

For me, the 'what' is to do with helping people to develop insights about their own living, and how they can develop their knowledge as a form of practice. I take pleasure in the idea that one's knowledge is constantly developing, and I encourage others to regard their thinking and practice as already good but always capable of modification and upgrading. This is an important issue in my main work contexts, where the culture is one which finds it hard to recognise excellence as a mark of responsible accountability rather than of arrogant self-aggrandisement. I like the evaluation of Paul Murphy of my own practice: 'Jean McNiff, my tutor, . . . demanded that I give according to my ability and was never satisfied with less' (Murphy, 2000: ii). I think it is important to demand of others according to their ability, and not be satisfied with less, provided one has the same expectations of oneself. In Senge's (1990: 4; emphasis in original) idea of how learning organisations may be characterised, 'The organizations that will truly excel in the future will be the organizations that discover how to tap people's commitment and capacity to learn at *all* levels in an organization.' I regard it as an ethical requirement that I struggle along with those I support, and also make my far from smooth process of coming to know public. It must not be assumed that all my encounters with course participants are easy. Sometimes there are clashes of opinion, personality, expectations; and it remains my responsibility to let others know that it is their responsibility, as well as mine, to work out our differences and move on.

Action research – what's in a name?

I do not think it matters what name we give to a concept as long as we all agree what we are talking about. As explained in Chapter 3, members of the action research family see action research in different ways, and they all call it action research. This situation is fine provided what one person says does not close down the opportunities for others also to have their say. In this book I am setting out my ideas, and also showing how critical reflection on their underpinning assumptions has led me to modify the ideas over time. While I respect the right of others to claim that their view of what counts as action research is a legitimate standpoint, I do require them to show their own critical reflection on the assumptions that inform their views. Otherwise, we get caught up in debates whose rules are arbitrary and reflect asymmetrical power relationships, and which reveal how some are explaining how they are living their values in their practice while others do not feel they have to.

I also want to say that, like Kevin McDermott (Chapter 12), I do not regard myself as an 'action researcher', in the sense that this is an identity, or that I am a member of a club. I dislike the idea of group identity; I have always resisted being corralled into one camp or another. This resistance to labelling also makes me not call myself a feminist, although I entirely agree with what feminists stand for. In normal usage we need terms and concepts as shorthand forms for effective communication; hence I write books about this idea which goes by the name of action research. That does not mean that I have the monopoly on truth about what action research is, but it does mean that I tell my truth as I see it. I do not believe that action research is a rigidly definable form of practice. I believe the term communicates values which I endorse, so to that extent I am prepared to engage with the ideas.

For me, it is all about Plato's questions of who we are, and how we are with one another. I believe, like Elton John, that we should never take more than we give; and for those in the privileged position of having the resources to think and act with relative freedom, it is our responsibility to give as much as is necessary in our efforts to tell the truth. This can be uncomfortable at times. If we are going to talk about action research and good social orders we need to step into the light of day and show how we are prepared to live out our rhetoric in our practice, otherwise we should be silent about these matters.

14 Significance of the work

Action research reports need to explain the significance of the work in terms of its potential for personal practice, institutional influence and the wider body of educational knowledge. This chapter does this as part of my research report.

Potentials for personal practice

The overall research question for my life work is 'How do I contribute to the development of a good social order through education?'

I have explained in Chapter 3 how the metaphors of unbounded generative transformational processes animate my view of personal–social enquiry. Each research project is itself a generative transformational process of enquiry which is part of wider generative transformational processes of enquiry. My overall research question embeds within itself more localised research questions such as 'How do I help this organisation to encourage more active public participation in decision-making?' or 'How do I help you to make sense of your practice?' Each project, however, is integrated within my own system of values as they manifest in my hope to contribute to social well-being at local and universal levels. No aspect of my work is separate from any other aspect, though sometimes I present it as such for clarity of analysis. Whatever happens in one area of life is bound to impact on another. My learning is transformative, my practice integrated.

At the same time I remember that the focus of the enquiry is me. I cannot take responsibility for anyone else. To think I could would be arrogant and educationally unsound. People are capable of making their own decisions, and need to if they are to be confident in their capacity to change personal and social situations. Definitions of action research everywhere emphasise that it is to bring about social change, which begins in individuals' minds. If action researchers are to effect change, the place to start is their own lives. Accepting the responsibility for one's own life and choices, however, can be very hard for some. John O'Donohue (2000: 145) speaks of the prisons we choose to live in, and those prisons include the way we think and 'the cage of frightened identity'. Erich Fromm described the same tendencies in his *Fear of Freedom* (1942). It is understandable that people are intimidated by the unknown, that we wish others to make choices and create our identities for us. If the world is to change, however, we have to do it ourselves. We might seek the advice and comfort of others who reassure us that we are making the right choices, but those choices ultimately have to be our own. And if they turn out to be the wrong ones, we also have to accept the responsibility of putting things right. There are, of course, people who are not able to make choices for reasons of pathology or coercion, and it is then the responsibility of those in positions of influence to support them and fight to arrange circumstances such that their voices are heard.

These are the kinds of broad values that today inform my work at a personal level. They have grown out of practice; I have learnt from experience (Winter, 1989). The experiential learning has been refined and extended by intellectual learning; the two are complementary, not separate, as many dominant theories would have us believe. My responsibility as a professional educator is to help people come to the same sorts of understandings about their lives. I am not here claiming that I have all the answers and am a model of good practice. I *am* claiming, however, that I am learning, which I believe is good practice, and my learning has led to social benefit. Learning has to begin in the individual mind – where else can it happen? – and learning of its nature is to be open to the possibilities of transforming present ideas into new ones. My work is in education, and I try to encourage people to see their capacity for good and take steps in new directions, and to offer emotional, intellectual, practical and political support to them as they progress. Professional learning which impacts on social situations, as action research does, is potentially hazardous as internal mental structures and external social structures are destabilised (see, for example, Buckley, 2000; Cahill, 2000), and people need to be encouraged to be tenacious, and be reassured that they will be supported through uncomfortable times.

My work as a professional educator has less to do with imparting a body of knowledge (as I thought in 1988) and everything to do with helping people to help themselves, by challenging and encouraging them to challenge their own assumptions and those of others; by caring for them in ways that they feel valued and supported in time of trouble; by not accepting less than their best; and by having faith and trust that they can do what they want to do. I think the shift in my own thinking and practice demonstrates a move from traditional E-theorising to the development of my own I-theory of education.

Potentials for workplace practice

Work, as Hannah Arendt (1990) and Christopher Mc Cormack (Chapter 9 of this book) tell us, is not labour. It is productive practice which contributes to our sense of identity. In this view work takes a variety of forms – mental, relational, practical – in a variety of places – the home, bus queues, industry. Work is never carried out in isolation, though it is often carried out alone. Paul Gray (2000: 99), for example, commenting on the work of Saul Bellow, speaks of writers as 'alone in rooms, filling up blank pages'. The impact of those words can, however, influence countless others to change their lives. When we work, we are always in relation with others, though they might be distant in time and space. Even what are often regarded as the most abstract of concepts, such as 'information' and 'the economy', are not abstract but refer to people interacting with one another. Information can be people exchanging and developing ideas (Castells, 1997); an economy can be people interacting to fulfil one another's needs (Henderson, 1996; Hutton, 1996).

Similarly, workplace practices refer to the processes whereby people exchange and develop ideas and interact with one another. Practices, however, are always informed by values. When practices are informed by the values of greed and personal aggrandisement, the practices become those of the selfish accumulation of resources by which people positioned as superior to others maintain their power. When the practices are informed by the values of tolerance and freedom, the practices become those of the shared knowledge of people participating on an equal footing in exercising their personal and collective choices about how they wish to create their identities.

There is considerable debate in the literatures of sociology and political science about whether it is possible for one person to influence wider social change. I do not see any other way. Social change is not an abstract concept; it is a lived process of people interacting and doing things differently from before, an everyday process of real life. When a person decides to shop at one supermarket rather than another, this is a factor of social change.

However, the dynamic of the relationships between individuals and the systems (themselves constituted of relationships) that others subscribe to can be problematic. Relationships between people, say Berlin (1998) and Gray (1995b) and the new theorists of discourse (see Torfing, 1999), are always potentially politically constructed. Even when two people come into contact a process of persuasion can develop (in extreme forms this can manifest as domination). Individuals are persuaded to become the people other people want them to be.

In an action research reading each person is capable of recreating themselves as the person they wish to be in negotiation with others; they need not necessarily conform to outmoded practices or expectations. In professional contexts such personal decision-making can be highly effective. Margaret Cahill (2000), for example, tells how she withstood considerable institutional pressure to prevent her from developing her practice in what she understood as educational ways. History is full of the stories of heroes and heroines who refused to give in to external pressure to conform. 'The hero is the opposite to the fatalist: he [*sic*] is on the side of the revolutionary, never the conservative, for he has no particular respect for the status quo and believes people can achieve any goal they choose, provided they have the will to do so' (Todorov, 1999: 5). It is well to remember, however, that in Dewey's view the idea of heroic self-recreation through personal decision-making from a kind of Nietzschean perspective is not appropriate in education or educational research. Education refers to a process of people interacting for mutual benefit, and encouraging development towards the good. Personal decisions always need to be made from within the contexts of social evolution, when the litmus test is the sustainable welfare of the most vulnerable member of a particular society as a contributor to its growth.

When these ideas are realised in practice they can generate amazing change. Let me take the dissertation work (for which she was awarded a distinction) of

Caitríona Mc Donagh as an example. Studying her practice as a learning support teacher, she (2000: 6) explains how she resisted dominant ideas that children were unproblematically categorised as 'dyslexic' or 'reading deficient':

> Three years ago, when I was appointed as a learning support teacher in my school, I decided to focus on my concern that, despite my best efforts, such pupils had not made the expected progress in norm references tests. I also questioned if my teaching could address their underlying difficulties. This dissertation was planned to address the idea that if my pupils could not learn using the form of thinking that I use when I teach, could I discover their thinking on learning, and could I adjust my teaching to accommodate it? In other words, since my pupils didn't learn to read and write in the way in which I taught, could I learn to teach in the way in which they learned?

She goes on to show that she did learn to teach in such a way that her pupils learned, and how she achieved this.

This is a good example of how one person's determination to change existing systems of knowledge and practice impacts on wider practices. Later, Caitríona (Mc Donagh, 2000: 72) writes:

> I believe that class teachers involved in this project benefited from a greater awareness and understanding of dyslexia. This could be evidenced in the addition of expressive and receptive language tutorials to the curriculum of a local voluntary workshop for children with dyslexia. This change occurred on the advice of a tutor who was also a colleague closely connected with my research.

She also writes, 'I believe that the full significance of my work is not the published end paper but the living interdependent growing initiatives it began in [the different areas of school life]' (p. 76).

Hero innovators (Rosser, n.d.), however, should never be naive or foolhardy. They should not believe that they achieve educational gains entirely on their own or without due recognition of the potential danger of institutional resistance. 'I encountered some teachers who still considered themselves gatekeepers of knowledge and were not open to change' (Mc Donagh, 2000: 79). How we deal with gatekeeping and arrange our own supports is also a matter of personal decision-making, which can especially benefit from the support of managers, as they exercise their responsibility as professional educators. People need to come together in community to build up their individual and corporate intellectual defences against efforts to close down their learning, and to press on with their educational and social intent.

This I believe is the way to develop learning organisations in the sense expressed by Senge (1990: 4) that all participants at all levels of workplaces need to learn. What they learn is at issue: knowledge for what?

> The peer support I experienced during the course of this research gave rise to a new confidence in me. In the past I had viewed colleagues in terms of their

positions in schools and colleges. I naively considered a class teacher inferior to a college lecturer. During this project, I came to value them as people. This encouraged me to propose changes in a spirit of community and support. My long held practices were destabilised following reflection. I found a methodology, which created a context of discovery and ways to move forward.

(Mc Donagh, 2000: 81)

I like to think that I have contributed to the development of a learning community among the participants I support. The reports and dissertations that course members produce show how I have encouraged them to think and act independently and interdependently in order to realise their own potentials for personal and institutional change. The network of practitioners so engaged has become a powerful force in Irish education contexts (see, for example, Hanafin and Leonard, 1996; Leonard, 1996; McNiff *et al.*, 2000). Perhaps a key reason for its potential as an educationally transformative organisation – a collection of people who aim to act collaboratively in order to realise collectively agreed educational values for social benefit – is that we are all open to our own learning, as Senge says. 'Never underestimate the power of groups of committed citizens to change the world. In fact, it is the only thing that ever has' (Mead, 1973, cited in Henderson, 1996: 123).

It does, though, all begin in the individual mind. Mc Donagh (2000: 80–1) ends her dissertation:

The joy of this research was that changes occurred like a waltz in the double motion of a dance between pupil development and my own learning . . . [The report is] an account of my own learning. I have discovered that educational theory can best be understood by developing my own theory. And the form of action research I chose facilitated this. It renewed in me – weary from a quarter of a century of teaching – the enthusiasm which drew me into teaching originally.

The same might also be experienced by those who are not content to be action research watchers but prefer to do action research as a lived practice and make their research findings public.

Potentials for educational theory

Ernest Boyer, when director of the Carnegie Foundation, spoke of the need for US universities to focus on teaching for learning, and to arrange for the systematic ongoing professional learning of university faculty (Boyer, 1990, 1991). University work, he says, should be about real-life teaching for learning, not only the generation of learned papers produced within traditional forms of scholarship. Developing the theme, Donald Schön (1995) explains that this focus on teaching for learning requires a new scholarship, one which is located within practice and which shows the reality of practical theorising.

What is studied in traditional scholarship are concrete subject matters and their accompanying bodies of literature. It is assumed that the theories contained therein can be universally applied to practice. Once the theories are applied, as a form of input, certain behaviours will occur, as a form of output. These behaviours can be manipulated as variables and their validity as acceptable forms can be tested using the standardised methods of traditional scientific approaches. What is studied in the new scholarship is personal practice, and theories are generated about the practice from within the practice. Practitioners are required to account for their practice by producing reports to show that they can explain how their work has improved in terms of enhancing the quality of learning and experience for themselves and others. The reports may be presented via multiple forms – written, oral, visual or combinations of these. Such accounts appear in this book; the book itself is such an account, a personal theory of practice.

A serious implication is that a new focus is developing in what counts as educational theory. Increasingly theory is being theorised as embodied in the lives of real practitioners, a systematically increasing focus on I-theories. This also has considerable political implications. Theory is now within the remit of all, and, if so, is no longer the province only of those positioned as knowledge workers at the Academy. All practitioners are potentially knowledge workers, capable of generating valid theory and having that theory recognised as legitimate within all personal or professional forums.

> The awesome respect in which I had held educational research and theories prior to my engagement with this project has given way to a new critical understanding of dilemmas of practice and theory. Living through the contradictions that arose has led me to appreciate the words of Elliott: 'Theoretical abstraction plays a subordinate role in the development of practical wisdom grounded in reflective experiences of concrete cases' (Elliott, 1991: 53) . . .
>
> Prior to this project I would not have considered my educational values or epistemology of practice worth sharing within the institution of the school. Living through the process of this research I have found a voice in the educational world. This teacher voice was seldom heard. The practising teacher tended to bow to academic educational theorists, to psychologists, to departmental inspectors, to parent bodies, yet where is the teacher's voice heard? Teacher craft was not valued by institutions of education professionals. This form of research has given colleagues and me a voice and method to articulate our theories.
>
> (Mc Donagh, 2000: 75, 81)

Are we contributing to the evolution of a good social order through education?

Good social orders are those in which all people may make their contribution and have it valued. In this view all are potential contributors, and all may participate in public debate and decision-making. The university is to be found in supermarkets as much as in traditional halls of learning. Knowledge is what people generate as they interact with one another for mutual benefit.

Let me return to the questions which have formed the organising principles for this book: What do I/we know? How do I/we come to know? What do I/we need to do? What do I/we need to know? What is my/our knowledge for?

I have produced my own report on knowledge, as it is constituted in this research report, this book. I have produced a book which attempts to show in practice the ideas it is aiming to communicate in words. In this sense the book is part of my own ongoing practice; it shows the development of my own living theory of education. You may accept it in part or whole; you may draw from it whatever might help you in your own learning.

By sharing our practice, critiquing and learning from one another, I believe we are developing new forms of educational theory which are squarely rooted in the experienced reality of people's lives. Traditional forms are embedded within and transcended by newer forms, and those newer forms contain the potential already to be developing in yet newer forms as our changing life circumstances direct.

I believe that it is the responsibility of all citizens, and particularly those positioned as public intellectuals – academics, managers, professional educators – to make our research reports available for public scrutiny, and to show how our theories are generated from within our creative and problematic practices as we try to make our educational visions come true for social good.

Epilogue

An educative conversation

Jean McNiff and Jack Whitehead

Jack It was great reading the final draft and seeing how you had tightened up the ideas. I've grown accustomed to this now. In your first drafts you tend to write spontaneously, often without critique. Then you go through with a critical eye and knock out the wilder statements.

Jean I've learnt this from you. I've learnt how to step back, to reflect on what I am writing, and to see whether it makes sense to a reader. These days I always write with a reader in mind. When I come to reading what I have written, if I don't understand it or if it doesn't read easily, I do it again. It doesn't matter how many drafts it takes.

Jack You've moved from the absolutist stance you used to have to a much more critical perspective, that's for sure. What I see myself doing as I respond to your writing is to draw attention to that tendency of yours to use assertions about 'all' without evidence. Over the years I've seen you work on this so that it is almost completely eliminated from your writing. Where it appeared in your present writing, I've drawn attention to it. If you think my points are justified it might be helpful to readers for them to see how you modify some of your thinking in relation to my responses. I think this would communicate something of the quality of our learning relationship.

Jean Like when I wrote something about the hubristic attitudes and ontologically bankrupt practices of researchers who position themselves as watchers rather than doers. You wrote to me, 'You may want to retain the emotional force of this criticism . . .' That means I should watch out because what I have written could be offensive and I need to edit it.

Jack Mmm. The other points where I think I've been useful over the years is in asking you to check the validity of some of the statements you make. For instance, in the present text I think I may have helped you to avoid making a mistake in writing about Ryle's work. I see in the final draft that you've rewritten that. I think I might have helped on ideas on epistemology. There is something in the way we've worked together which has enabled us to value each other's creativity and to help to take each other's ideas forward. I reckon we understand better this learning process than we did in 1988!

Jean I am aware of how much I have learnt from you. I always feel I take more than I give. I used to think: What can Jack possibly learn from me? In a substantive sense you know far more than I do about research issues. You have read far more widely than I have in these areas. You have a deep background in philosophy and the history of ideas. I feel almost that I've only recently begun in these areas. My formative years were spent reading westerns. I read *Gone with the Wind* in a four-day sitting when I was twelve.

Jack   I learn other things from you. I have observed how you are with people, how you communicate the passion of your ideas without imposing them on others. I have seen how you inspire others to do their best, how you manage to build community through educative relationships. I am practising the same in my work.

I also understand better the concept of emotional literacy through working with you. Earlier today I pointed out that you might have been mistaken in your ideas about the form of explanations people offer. I think the way you responded demonstrated emotional maturity. You were able to be open to my critique without becoming defensive. You were able to see that you were making judgements from within your own terms of reference. You saw this and immediately said that you were doing what you were criticising others for doing.

And you have read widely in other areas, too, and I have learnt from you. As I read this text I feel the growth of my insights into Noam Chomsky's ideas as I engage with your own creative appreciation of the value of his work for your own. Your writings also focus my attention on the importance of explaining the differences between propositional and living forms of educational theory in ways which integrate useful insights from the propositional theories in the creation and testing of living educational theories. I also like the way you address the ideas of others in terms of their influence on your thinking. What I learn from you, among other things, is how I need to refine my own ideas and communicate them clearly.

Jean   I'm going back to being dogmatic for a moment, when I say that I am quite sure I would never have done what I have done without knowing that you were there in the background. There are certain people who provide stable points of reference for my life. You are one of them. I remember when I attended the seminar to transfer from MPhil to PhD. I told the committee about all the things that were happening in my classroom because I had started thinking about what I was doing. One of the committee said, 'How do you know all these things wouldn't have happened without you?' You and I had rehearsed the seminar beforehand, and you had asked me this, and I had worked out what was involved in the question so now knew what to answer, and I said, 'I don't, but I do know they are happening with me.' Now, I know that if you hadn't been there I would have continued to teach, and would also probably have gone on to write. But life would never have been so rich because the ideas would not have been developed and refined through the learning and the critique, and, for me, ideas are often more important than food or money. I do know that I am living a life which I want to live, and helping others to do the same.

Be aware that I am saying this from a perspective which took time to develop. You were my supervisor, my tutor, and in a sense it was an adult–child relationship. I often experience this with people whom I supervise. It is quite wonderful when you develop an adult–adult relationship. You can speak your own ideas without fear that the other will be intimidated. It took me time to grow in the relationship with you, to see myself as a learning equal. While we might have different backgrounds and different contexts, we are both teachers and both learners, and that perhaps is what is at the heart of the matter. We are both open to learning.

Appendix

Connecting with other communities of enquirers

It is important that you should feel connected with other people who are pursuing their action enquiries. Try to get connected to networks locally and internationally. Being connected will give you support and help you to keep up to date with developments in the field, as well as providing a critical forum to test your ideas and create new ones.

Local communities can build up through the efforts of one person (possibly you) contacting others and suggesting that you form a research group. You could approach the people in your own existing study group, if you are on a course, or in your workplace. Enlisting the help of a senior manager can be useful. If you can't arrange face-to-face meetings with your local group, try to build up a support group using electronic communications. You could develop an e-group, for example.

Try to make connections with the international communities. Seek out and attend conferences. Try also to find opportunities to present your work publicly, both as text and also through live presentation.

Getting connected

The easiest way to get connected is to access http://www.actionresearch.net. This website contains the dissertations and theses of many researchers who have gained their higher degrees with Jack Whitehead through the University of Bath, as well as forums for keeping up to date with progress in the world of action research. The 'other homepages' section will also put you in touch immediately with other major websites around the world.

At time of writing, we would suggest you make every effort to connect with the following:

*   Action Research in Oregon at:
    http://beta.open.k12.or.us/arowhelp/

*   Action Research Resources at Southern Cross University at:
    http://www.scu.edu.au/schools/gcm/ar/arhome.html

- Centre for Action Research in Professional Practice (CARPP) at:
  http://www.bath.ac.uk/management/carpp/

- The Collaborative Action Research Network (CARN) at:
  http://www.uea.ac.uk/care/carn/

- International Teacher Research Organization at:
  http://www.teacherresearch.org

- Jean McNiff at:
  http://www.jeanmcniff.com

- Self-Study of Teacher Education Practices - A special interest group of the American Educational Research Association at:
  http://www.educ.ubc.ca/faculty/lstanley/te/

References

Airasian, P. W. (1996) *Assessment in the Classroom.* New York, McGraw-Hill.

Anderson, G. L. and Herr, K. (1999) 'The new paradigm wars: Is there room for rigorous practitioner knowledge in schools and universities?', *Educational Researcher* 28(5): 12–21.

Arendt, H. (1990) *On Revolution.* London, Penguin Books.

Atkinson, E. (2000) 'Behind the Inquiring Mind: Exploring the transition from external to internal inquiry', *Reflective Practice* 1(2): 149–64.

Atweh, B., Kemmis. S. and Weeks, P. (1998) *Action Research in Practice: Partnerships for Social Justice in Education.* London, Routledge.

Bakhtin, M. M. (1986) *Speech Genres and Other Late Essays*, ed. C. Emerson and M. Holquist, trans. V. W. McGee. Austin, University of Texas Press.

Ball, S. J. (1987) *The Micropolitics of the School.* London, Routledge.

Ball, S. J. (1990) *Foucault and Education: Disciplines and Knowledge.* London, Routledge.

Bassey, M. (1999) *Case Study Research in Educational Settings.* Buckingham, Open University Press.

Bateson, M. C. (1994) *Peripheral Visions: Learning along the Way.* New York, Harper-Collins.

Bell, J. (1993) *Doing Your Research Project: A Guide for First-time Researchers in Education and Social Science* (second edition). Buckingham, Open University Press.

Bell, B., Gaventa, J. and Peters, J. (1990) *We Make the Road by Walking: Myles Horton and Paolo Freire, Conversations on Education and Social Change.* Philadelphia, Temple University Press.

Berlin, I. (1998) *The Proper Study of Mankind: An Anthology of Essays.* London, Pimlico.

Boal, A. (1992) *Games for Actors and Non-actors.* London, Routledge.

Bohm, D. (1983) *Wholeness and the Implicate Order.* London, Ark Paperbacks.

Bohm, D. and Peat, F. D. (2000) *Science, Order and Creativity* (second edition). London, Routledge.

Bourdieu, P. (1990) *The Logic of Practice.* London, Polity Press.

Bourdieu, P. (1993) *Sociology in Question.* London, Sage.

Boyer, E. (1990) *Scholarship Reconsidered: Priorities of the Professoriate.* New Jersey, Carnegie Foundation for the Advancement of Teaching.

Boyer, E. (1991) 'Seasonal work for creative professoriate', *Times Higher Education Supplement,* 28 June: 19.

Broadfoot, P. (1979) *Assessment, Schools and Society.* London, Methuen.

Bryk, A., Lee, V. and Holland, P. (1993) *Catholic Schools and the Common Good.* Cambridge, Mass., Harvard University Press.

Buber, M. (1937) *I and Thou*, trans. R. G. Smith. Edinburgh, T. & T. Clark.

Buckley, M. J. (2000) 'How can I improve my practice by using creative writing?', unpublished MA dissertation, Cork, University of the West of England, Bristol.

Cahill, M. (2000) 'How can I encourage pupils to participate in their own learning?', unpublished MA dissertation, Thurles, University of the West of England, Bristol.

Capra, F., Steindl-Rast, D. with T. Matus (1992) *Belonging to the Universe: New Thinking about God and Nature.* London, Penguin.

Carr, W. and Kemmis, S. (1986) *Becoming Critical: Education, Knowledge and Action Research.* London, Falmer.

Carson, T. R. and Sumara, D. J. (eds) (1997) *Action Research as a Living Practice.* New York, Peter Lang Publishing.

Castells, M. (1997) *The Rise of the Network Society* (Vol. 1). Oxford, Blackwell.

Chomsky, N. (1965) *Aspects of the Theory of Syntax.* Cambridge, Mass., Massachusetts Institute of Technology.

Chomsky, N. (1966) 'The responsibility of intellectuals', reprinted in N. Chomsky (1988) *The Chomsky Reader*, ed. J. Peck. London, Serpent's Tail.

Chomsky, N. (1986) *Knowledge of Language: Its Nature, Origin and Use.* New York, Praeger.

Chomsky, N. (1996) *Power and Prospects: Reflections on Human Nature and the Social Order.* London, Pluto.

Chomsky, N. (2000) *New Horizons in the Study of Language and Mind.* Cambridge, Cambridge University Press.

Clarke, C. (2000) 'Improving discipline through educative relationships', unpublished working paper, Treforest, University of Glamorgan.

Collier, J. (1945) 'United States Indian administration as a laboratory of ethnic relations', *Social Research* 12: 265–303.

Collins, Ú. M. and McNiff, J. (eds) (1999) *Rethinking Pastoral Care.* London, Routledge.

Condren, D. (2000) 'The Mol an Óige Project' in J. McNiff, G. McNamara and D. Leonard (eds), *Action Research in Ireland.* Dorset, September Books.

Corey, S. (1953) *Action Research to Improve School Practices.* New York, Teachers College.

D'Arcy, P. (1998) 'The Whole Story . . .', unpublished Ph.D. thesis, University of Bath, www.actionresearch.net.

Davies, L. (1990) *Equity and Efficiency? School Management in an International Context.* London, Falmer.

Davies, P. (1992) 'Is the universe a machine?' in N. Hall (ed.), *The 'New Scientist' Guide to Chaos.* London, Penguin.

Dawkins, R. (1987) *The Blind Watchmaker.* New York, Norton.

Delong, J. (2000) 'My epistemology of practice of the superintendency' in J. McNiff, *Action Research in Organisations.* London, Routledge.

Dewey, J. (1916) *Democracy and Education.* New York, Free Press.

Dodd, D. (2001) 'Improving the quality of education at an adult education centre', unpublished MA dissertation, Dublin, University of the West of England, Bristol.

Ebbutt, D. (1985) 'Educational action research: Some general concerns and specific quibbles' in R. Burgess (ed.), *Issues in Educational Research.* London, Falmer.

Ebbutt, D. and Elliott, J. (eds) (1985) *Issues in Teaching for Understanding.* London, Longman/Schools Curriculum Development Committee.

Eden, C. and Huxham, C. (1999) 'Action research for the study of organizations' in S. Clegg and C. Hardy (eds), *Studying Organization: Theory and Method.* London, Sage.

Elliott, J. (1991) *Action Research for Educational Change.* Buckingham, Open University Press.

Elliott, J. (1998) *The Curriculum Experiment: Meeting the Challenge of Social Change.* Buckingham, Open University Press.

Ernest, P. (1994) *An Introduction to Research Methodology and Paradigms.* Exeter, University of Exeter Research Support Unit.

Evans, M. (1996) 'An action research inquiry into reflection in action as part of my role as a deputy headteacher', unpublished Ph.D. thesis, University of Kingston.

Feynman, R. (1999) *The Meaning of It All.* London, Penguin.

Field, J. and Leicester, M. (2000) *Lifelong Learning: Education across the Lifespan.* London, RoutledgeFalmer.

Foucault, M. (1980) 'Truth and Power' in C. Gordon (ed.), *Power/Knowledge: Selected Interviews and Other Writings, 1972–1977.* Brighton, Harvester.

Fox, S. (1997) 'From management education and development to the study of management learning' in J. Burgoyne and M. Reynolds (eds), *Management Learning: Integrating Perspectives in Theory and Practice.* London, Sage.

Fromm, E. (1942) *Fear of Freedom.* London, Routledge and Kegan Paul.

Fromm, E. (1956) *The Art of Loving,* World Perspectives (Vol. 9). New York, Harper & Row.

Fullan, M. (1992) *Successful School Improvement.* Buckingham, Open University Press.

Gardner, J. (1983) *Frames of Mind: The Theory of Multiple Intelligences.* New York, Basic Books.

Gipps, C. V. (1994) *Towards a Theory of Educational Assessment.* London, Falmer.

Golding, D. and Currie, D. (2000) *Thinking about Management: A Reflective Practice Approach.* London, Routledge.

Government of Ireland (1996) *Transition Year Programmes Guidelines for Schools.* Dublin, Stationery Office.

Government of Ireland (1998) *School Development Planning.* Dublin, Stationery Office.

Government of Ireland (1999a) *Whole School Evaluation: Report on the 1998/1999 Pilot Project.* Dublin, Stationery Office.

Government of Ireland (1999b) *Primary School Curriculum: Introduction.* Dublin, Stationery Office.

Grace, G. (1995) *School Leadership: Beyond Education Management. An Essay in Policy Scholarship.* London, Falmer.

Gray, J. (1995a) *Berlin.* London, Fontana.

Gray, J. (1995b) *Enlightenment's Wake: Politics and Culture at the Close of the Modern Age.* London, Routledge.

Gray, P. (2000) 'Bellow the word king', *Time,* 20 November: 99.

Habermas, J. (1972) *Knowledge and Human Interests,* trans. J. J. Shapiro. London, Heinemann.

Habermas, J. (1973) *Legitimation Crisis,* trans. T. McCarthy. Boston, Beacon Press.

Habermas, J. (1974) *Theory and Practice,* trans. J. Viertel. London, Heinemann.

Habermas, J. (1979) *Communication and the Evolution of Society,* trans. T. McCarthy. Boston, Beacon Press.

Habermas, J. (1990) *Moral Consciousness and Communicative Action.* Cambridge, Mass., MIT Press.

Hadfield, M. (1998) 'Review of T. R. Carson and D. J. Sumara (eds) *Action Research as a Living Practice*', *Educational Action Research* 6(3): 536–8.

Hamilton, M. L. (ed.) (1998) *Reconceptualizing Teaching Practice: Self-study in Teacher Education.* London, Falmer.

Hanafin, J. and Leonard, D. (1996) 'Conceptualising and implementing quality: Assessment and the Junior Certificate', *Irish Educational Studies* 15: 26–39.

Hargreaves, D. (1996) *Teaching as a Research-based Profession: Possibilities and Prospects.* Teacher Training Agency Annual Lecture, Teacher Training Agency, London.

Hausheer, R. (1998) 'Introduction' in I. Berlin, *The Proper Study of Mankind: An Anthology of Essays.* London, Pimlico.

Henderson, H. (1996) *Building a Win–Win World: Life beyond Global Economic Warfare.* San Francisco, Berrett-Koehler.

Higgins, A. (2000) 'Action research: A means of changing and improving the clinical learning environment' in J. McNiff, G. McNamara and D. Leonard (eds), *Action Research in Ireland.* Dorset, September Books.

Hitchcock, G. and Hughes, D. (1995) *Research and the Teacher: A Qualitative Introduction to School-based Research* (second edition). London, Routledge.

Hogan, P. (2000) 'The road not taken and the one with better claim', *Issues in Education – Teaching as a Profession.* Dublin, Association of Secondary Teachers, Ireland: 13–20.

Hoyle, E. (1974) 'Professionality, professionalism and control in teaching', *London Educational Review* 3(2).

Hoyle, E. and John, P. (1995) *Professional Knowledge and Professional Practice.* London, Cassell.

Hutton, W. (1996) *The State We're In.* London, Vintage.

Hyland, Á. (ed.) (1998) *Innovations in Assessment in Irish Education: Multiple Intelligences, Curriculum and Assessment Project.* Education Department, University College, Cork.

James, G. (1991) *Quality of Working Life and Total Quality Management*, Work Research Unit Occasional Paper No. 50. London, ACAS, WRU.

Jenkins, R. (1992) *Pierre Bourdieu.* London, Routledge.

Kemmis, S. (1993) 'Action research' in M. Hammersley (ed.), *Educational Research: Current Issues.* London, Paul Chapman with the Open University.

Kemmis, S. and McTaggart, R. (1982) *The Action Research Planner* (first edition). Geelong, Deakin University Press.

Kemmis, S. and McTaggart, R. (1988) *The Action Research Planner* (third edition). Geelong, Deakin University Press.

Kingore, B. (1993) *Enriching and Assessing All Students – Identifying the Gifted Grades K–6.* Iowa, Leadership Publishers.

Kuhn, T. (1970) *The Structure of Scientific Revolutions* (second edition). Chicago, University of Chicago Press.

Laidlaw, M. (1996) 'How can I create my own living educational theory through accounting to you for my own educational development?', unpublished Ph.D. thesis, University of Bath.

Leonard, D. (1996) 'Quality in education and teacher development', *Irish Educational Studies* 15: 56–67.

Lewin, K. (1946) 'Action research and minority problems', *Journal of Social Issues* 2(4): 34–46.

Lillis, C. (2000a) 'Reclaiming school as a caring place' in J. McNiff, G. McNamara and D. Leonard (eds), *Action Research in Ireland.* Dorset, September Books.

Lillis, C. (2000b) 'How one school is fulfilling Peter Senge's vision of the "learning organisation"' in J. McNiff, *Action Research in Organisations.* London, Routledge.

Lomax, P. (1994) *The Narrative of an Educational Journey or Crossing the Track.* Inaugural lecture, Kingston, University of Kingston.

Lomax, P. (ed.) (1996) *Quality Management in Education.* London, Routledge.

Lomax, P. (1999) 'Working together for educative community through research'. Presidential address, BERA Annual Conference, Belfast, August. Reprinted in *British Educational Research Journal* 25(1): 5–21.

Lomax, P., Evans, M., Parker, Z. and Whitehead, J. (1999) 'Knowing ourselves as teacher educators: Joint self-study through electronic mail', *Educational Action Research* 7(2): 235–57.

Lynch, K. (2000) 'Equality studies, the Academy and the role of research in emancipatory social change' in J. McNiff, G. McNamara and D. Leonard (eds), *Action Research in Ireland*. Dorset, September Books. (Originally published in the *Economic and Social Review* 30(1): 41–69.)

Lyons, J. (1970) *Chomsky*. London, Fontana.

Lyotard, J.-F. (1984) *The Postmodern Condition: A Report on Knowledge*, trans. G. Bennington and B. Massumi. Manchester, Manchester University Press.

McDermott, K. (2000) 'Reading practice: Essays in dialogue and pedagogical conversation', unpublished working paper, Treforest, University of Glamorgan.

Mc Donagh, C. (2000) 'Towards a theory of a professional teacher voice: How can I improve my teaching of pupils with specific learning difficulties in the area of language?', unpublished MA dissertation, Dublin, University of the West of England, Bristol.

MacDonald, B. and Walker, R. (1976) *Changing the Curriculum*. London, Open Books.

MacIntyre, A. (1990) *Three Rival Versions of Moral Enquiry: Encyclopaedia, Genealogy, Tradition*. Guildford, Duckworth.

McKernan, J. (1991) *Curriculum Action Research: A Handbook of Methods and Resources for the Reflective Practitioner*. London, Kogan Page.

McNamara, G. and O'Hara, J. (2000) 'Action research for organisational change' in J. McNiff, G. McNamara and D. Leonard (eds), *Action Research in Ireland*. Dorset, September Books.

McNiff, J. (1993) *Teaching as Learning: An Action Research Approach*. London, Routledge.

McNiff, J. (2001) 'Evaluating the educational impact of information and communications technology in Irish schools'. Paper presented at the International Conference for Teacher Research, Richmond, British Columbia, April.

McNiff, J. with J. Whitehead (2000) *Action Research in Organisations*. London, Routledge.

McNiff, J. and Collins, Ú. (eds) (1994) *A New Approach to In-career Development for Teachers in Ireland*. Bournemouth, Hyde.

McNiff, J., Lomax, P. and Whitehead, J. (1996) *You and Your Action Research Project*. London, Routledge.

McNiff, J., McNamara, G. and Leonard, D. (eds) (2000) *Action Research in Ireland*. Dorset, September Books.

Martin, M. (1997) Speech at the Launch of *Schools IT2000*, Dublin.

Mead, M. (1973) 'Our open-ended future' in *The Next Billion Years*. Lecture Series at the University of California, Los Angeles.

Mellor, N. (1998) 'Notes from a method', *Educational Action Research*, 6(3): 453–70.

Murdoch, I. (1985) *The Sovereignty of Good*. London, Ark Paperbacks.

Murphy, P. (2000) 'How I developed a practice and learned to conduct it more effectively', unpublished MA dissertation, Dublin, University of the West of England, Bristol.

Newby, M. (1994) 'Living theory or living contradiction?, a review essay of J. McNiff's *Teaching as Learning: An Action Research Approach*, London, Routledge (1993)', *Journal of Philosophy of Education* 28(1): 119–26.

Ní Mhurchú, S. (1999) 'Describe and evaluate the main features of an action research approach to educational enquiry, and critically assess the potential contribution such an approach could make to your educational practice.' Assignment for the MA in Education programme, Cork, University of the West of England, Bristol.

Ní Mhurchú, S. (2000) 'How can I improve my practice as a teacher in the area of assessment through the use of portfolios?', unpublished MA dissertation, Cork, University of the West of England, Bristol.

Noffke, S. (1997a) 'Themes and tensions in US action research: Towards historical analysis' in S. Hollingsworth (ed.), *International Action Research: A Casebook for Educational Reform*. London, Falmer.

Noffke, S. (1997b) *Professional, Personal, and Political Dimensions of Action Research: The 1997 Review of Educational Research* (Vol. 22). Washington, American Educational Research Association.

Nugent, M. (2000) 'How can I raise the level of self-esteem of second year Junior Certificate School Programme students and create a better learning environment?', unpublished MA dissertation, Dublin, University of the West of England, Bristol.

O'Brien, O. (2000) 'Planning for the future' in CORI Pastoral Commission (eds), *Religious in Parish: Reflecting on the Experience, Directions for the Future*. Dublin, CORI Publications.

O'Donohue, J. (2000) *Eternal Echoes: Exploring our Hunger to Belong*. London, Bantam Books.

Ó Muimhneacháin, C. (1999) 'A critical analysis of the potential contribution of an action research apoproach to educational enquiry and practice', unpublished assignment for the MA in Education programme, Cork, University of the West of England, Bristol.

O'Neill, R. (2000) 'The Setanta Project – developing a school subject-based intranet'. Paper presented at the SIP Symposium, Portmarnock, Dublin, 2 December.

O'Neill, R. (2001) 'An approach to ICTs as part of organisational change', unpublished working paper, Treforest, University of Glamorgan.

Open University Course E811 (1988) *Educational Evaluation*. Buckingham, Open University Educational Enterprises.

O'Shea, K. (2000) 'Coming to know my own practice', unpublished MA dissertation, Dublin, University of the West of England, Bristol

Parlett, M. and Hamilton, D. (1976) 'Evaluation as illumination: A new approach to the study of innovatory programmes' in D. A. Tawney (ed.), *Curriculum Evaluation Today: Trends and Implications*. Basingstoke, Macmillan Education.

Pettinger, R. (1999) *The Future of Industrial Relations*. London, Continuum.

Polanyi, M. (1958) *Personal Knowledge*. London, Routledge and Kegan Paul.

Polanyi, M. (1967) *The Tacit Dimension*. New York, Doubleday.

Pollard, A. (1997) *Reflective Teaching in the Primary School: A Handbook for the Classroom*. London, Cassell.

Pring, R. (2000) *Philosophy of Educational Research*. London, Continuum.

Prosser, J. (ed.) (1998) *Image-based Research: A Sourcebook for Qualitative Researchers*. London, Falmer.

Rizvi, F. (1989) 'In defence of organizational democracy' in J. Smyth (ed.), *Critical Perspectives on Educational Leadership*. London, Falmer.

Robson, C. (1993) *Real World Research: A Resource for Social Scientists and Practitioner-researchers*. Oxford, Blackwell.

Roche, M. (2000) 'How can I improve my practice so as to help my pupils to philosophise?', unpublished MA dissertation, Cork, University of the West of England, Bristol.

Rorty, R. (1999) *Philosophy and Social Hope*. London, Penguin.

Rosser, D. (n.d.) 'Eating hero-innovators is wrong', *Managing Development*, mimeo, University of the West of England, Bristol.

Rowan, J. and Reason, P. (1981) *Human Inquiry: A Sourcebook for New Paradigm Research.* Chichester, John Wiley & Sons.

Rudduck, J. and Hopkins, D. (eds) (1985) *Research as a Basis for Teaching.* London, Heinemann.

Ryle, G. (1949) *The Concept of Mind.* London, Hutchinson.

Said, E. (1991) *The World, the Text, and the Critic.* London, Vintage.

Said, E. (1995) *Orientalism.* London, Penguin.

Sanford, N. (1970) 'Whatever happened to action research?', *Journal of Social Issues,* 26: 3–13. Reprinted in S. Kemmis *et al.* (eds) (1982) *The Action Research Reader* (first edition). Geelong, Deakin University Press.

Schein, E. (1996) *Three Cultures of Management: The Key to Organisational Learning in the 21st Century,* Cambridge, Mass.: MIT Sloan School of Management.

Schön, D. (1983) *The Reflective Practitioner: How Professionals Think in Action.* New York, Basic Books.

Schön, D. (1995) 'Knowing-in-action: The new scholarship requires a new epistemology', *Change,* November–December: 27–34.

Schratz, M. (1998) 'Towards a new architecture of learning: Reflection on action as an experience of change'. Keynote address to the conference 'Action Research and the Politics of Educational Knowledge', Trinity College, Dublin. Reprinted in J. McNiff, G. McNamara and D. Leonard (eds) (2000) *Action Research in Ireland.* Dorset, September Books.

Schratz, M. and Steiner-Löffler, U. (1998) 'Pupils using photographs in school self-evaluation' in J. Prosser (ed.), *Image-based Research: A Sourcebook for Qualitative Researchers.* London, Falmer.

Schwab, J. J. (1969) 'The practical: A language for the curriculum', *School Review* 78: 1–24.

Senge, P. (1990) *The Fifth Discipline: The Art and Practice of the Learning Organization.* New York, Doubleday.

Slee, R., Weiner, G. with S. Tomlinson (eds) (1998) *School Effectiveness for Whom? Challenges to the School Effectiveness and School Improvement Movements.* London, Falmer.

Smyth, J. and Shacklock, G. (1998) *Re-making Teaching.* London, Routledge.

Sockett, H. (1993) *The Moral Base for Teacher Professionalism.* New York, Teachers College Press.

Sowell, T. (1987) *A Conflict of Visions: Ideological Origins of Political Struggles.* New York, Morrow.

Stenhouse, L. (1975) *An Introduction to Curriculum Research and Development.* London, Heinemann.

Strike, K. and Soltis, J. (1985) *The Ethics of Teaching.* New York, Teachers College Press.

Teacher Training Agency (1998) *National Standards for Qualified Teacher Status: Subject Leaders; Special Educational Needs Co-ordinators; Headteachers.* London, Teacher Training Agency.

Thomas, G. (1998) 'The myth of rational research', *British Educational Research Journal* 24(2): 141–61.

Todorov, T. (1999) *Facing the Extreme: Moral Life in the Concentration Camps.* London, Weidenfeld & Nicolson.

Torbert, W. (1981) 'Why educational research has been so uneducational: The case for a new model of social science based on collaborative inquiry' in P. Reason and J. Rowan (eds), *Human Inquiry: A Sourcebook for New Paradigm Research.* Chichester, John Wiley and Sons.

Torfing, J. (1999) *New Theories of Discourse: Laclau, Mouffe and Žižek.* Oxford, Oxford University Press.

Usher, R. (1996) 'A critique of the neglected epistemological assumptions of educational research' in D. Scott and R. Usher (eds), *Understanding Educational Research.* London, Routledge.

Vico, G. (1999 [1744]) *New Science*, trans. D. Marsh. London, Penguin.

Whitehead, J. (1985) 'An analysis of an individual's educational development: The basis for personally oriented action research' in M. Shipman (ed.), *Educational Research: Principles, Policies and Practice.* London, Falmer.

Whitehead, J. (1989) 'Creating a living educational theory from questions of the kind, "How do I improve my practice?"', *Cambridge Journal of Education* 19(1): 137–53.

Whitehead, J. (1993) *The Growth of Educational Knowledge: Creating Your Own Living Educational Theories.* Bournemouth, Hyde.

Whitehead, J. (1998) 'Developing research-based professionalism through living educational theories'. A keynote presentation to the conference 'Action Research and the Politics of Educational Knowledge', Trinity College, Dublin, November. Reprinted in J. McNiff, G. McNamara and D. Leonard (eds) (2000) *Action Research in Ireland.* Dorset, September Books.

Whitehead, J. (1999) 'Educative relations in a new era', *Pedagogy, Culture & Society* 7(1): 73–90.

Whitehead, J. (2000) 'How do I improve my practice? Creating and legitimating an epistemology of practice', *Reflective Practice* 1(1): 91–104.

Whitehead, J. (forthcoming) *Logics and Values of Living Educational Theories.*

Winter, R. (1989) *Learning from Experience: Principles and Practice in Action-research.* London, Falmer.

Winter, R. (1999) 'The University of Life plc: The "industrialization" of higher education' in J. Ahier and G. Esland (eds), *Education, Training and the Future of Work, Vol. 1: Social, Political and Economic Contexts of Policy Development.* London, Routledge and the Open University.

Young, M. F. D. (1998) *The Curriculum of the Future: From the 'New Sociology of Education' to a Critical Theory of Learning.* London, Falmer.

Zeichner, K. (1999) 'The new scholarship in teacher education', *Educational Researcher* 28(9): 4–15.

Žižek, S. (1990) 'Beyond discourse analysis' in E. Laclau (ed.), *New Reflections on the Revolution of Our Time.* London, Verso.

Zuber-Skerritt, O. (1992a) *Professional Development in Higher Education: A Theoretical Framework for Action Research.* London, Kogan Page.

Zuber-Skerritt, O. (1992b) *Action Research in Higher Education: Examples and Reflections.* London, Kogan Page.

Zuber-Skerritt, O. (1996) 'Emancipatory action research for organisational change and management development' in O. Zuber-Skerritt (ed.), *New Directions in Action Research.* London, Falmer.

Index